DRACONOMICON

MERLYN STONE'S LONG-LOST CLASSIC

DRACONOMICON

BOOK OF ANCIENT DRAGON MAGICK

by Joshua Free writing as Merlyn Stone
with Foreword by Rowen Gardner

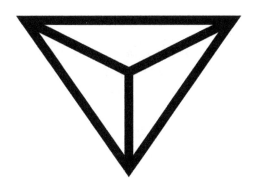

First published underground as a booklet.
Revised and expanded to form this
25th Anniversary Edition.

© 1995 – 2020, JOSHUA FREE
Second Printing—May 2020

ISBN : 978-0-578-53148-9

Being an investigation into the nature of the DRAGON throughout history; and the magic and traditions inspired by the same—so that those who might come seeking this True Knowledge shall not go away in wanting.

—TABLET OF CONTENTS—

FOREWORD TO THE 25TH ANNIVERSARY COLLECTOR'S EDITION

by Rowen Gardner

HERE BE DRAGONS! Behold the ultimate *"Book of the Dragon"* for modern magick-users and fantasy enthusiasts alike—now completely revised and expanded for its 25th anniversary. This underground cult-classic *"Draconomicon"* offers powerful teachings and lore of ancient "dragon magick" and its legacy.

Discovering true knowledge, wisdom and power of the Dragon has never been easier!

Joshua Free—a leading member of the occult underground for the past twenty-five years—provides seekers with a unique and remarkable treasury of esoteric knowledge in this new amazing collector's edition of what is sure to be the perfect addition to your library and/or "dragon collection."

Come and initiate yourself to the Ancient Mystery School and venture on a progressive journey through the *Dragon Legacy*—beginning in the depths of the Primordial Abyss and primeval birth of the "Great Cosmic Dragon" and following through the many millennium of secret knowledge carried to the present age...and the future! Whether you are simply curious, or seeking to explore deep teachings that may incorporate "dragons" into your spiritual and magical systems, the *Draconomicon* is unparalleled research and testimony to a quarter-of-a-century modern occult evolution, sparking hundreds of traditions.

The *Dragon Legacy* is an important and integral part of the history and traditions of <u>all</u> cultures, and subsequently underlies all cultural magical traditions—not to mention symbols and motifs that lie beneath the development of human civilization as a whole. *Nothing is separate.* And this is one of the lessons we learn from *The Dragon*—that everything is connected together and we cannot see things in exclusion to other things if we are to see things, *Self-honestly*, for how they truly are—another gift of *The Dragon*.

Hidden in the depths of the *Dragon's Lair* is an untold legacy of knowledge and power, secret societies and bloodlines, cults and symbols encompassing our entire material existence—and the means by which it can be controlled. It is quite possible this is among the best kept secrets in the history of occultism, even enshrouded in a cacophony of grand conspiracies. And in its most ancient forms, it is the undefiled, raw and primordial *Truth* of things—just as we would expect the Druids, wizards and sages of old to understand them. *And with understanding comes wisdom.*

As a resident—born and raised—in Wales, the Dragon has been a part of my life for as long as I can remember. But, I believe that the Dragon—its symbolism and energetic currents—most likely resonates strongest with many of those folk who feel a calling to esoteric, occult, fantasy and magical aspects of life. It is not much different, perhaps, from the inclination and interests that many similar types of people share with other elemental embodiments, for whatever the personal reasons may be, both known or unknown—be it garden gnomes or gargoyles, fairies or trolls, elves or unicorns. There is something uniquely familiar or nostalgic registering within us when we participate—and it is perhaps this *recognition* that, in part, supports a basis for bringing the *real magic* into our lives.

The presence of the Dragon may be felt everywhere on earth and throughout the cosmos, though what it means to each of us—the manner it *appears* in our daily lives—seems to adjust itself based on our cultural background and even our religion. It manifests as a *devil* to the uninitiated—those orthodox types too bound up in fears of western dogma to behold raw power of the dragon. It also manifests beautifully in the east, as the spirit of all natural creation, such as is maintained by *Mahayana Buddhists* residing between Tibet and India in the country of Bhutan or "Druk Yül"—the "Land of the Thunder Dragon."

The *Draconomicon* reflects a <u>holistic</u> approach to the "Dragon," a "systemology" that is uniquely present in all works by the author—and to which I am privileged the opportunity to add "more light" to for this edition. In many ways, and in spite of its ongoing evolution throughout its author's lifetime, the work is deserving of "more light." Genuine power inherent in the *Draconomicon* comes from a place in *Self* that most readers used to contemporary "New Age" puff-ball materials are at risk to overlook. And I believe this is equally the case concerning other tomes and volumes presented by Joshua Free since the mid-90's underground appearance of the *Draconomicon* in its original form.

Where many other books on "dragon magick" have appeared in the New Age marketplace, what we actually find is either a synthesis of variegated mythologies that simply share dragon semantics, or else a revised tradition of established ritual magic or "wiccan" elements that simply incorporate themes and names associated with dragons. If desired, the *Draconomicon* may be used to these same ends—but it is not its purpose. In fact, as with many original inceptions of its author's works, the *Draconomicon* was not written or intended for "mass circulation," first released underground under the pseudonym of "*Merlyn Stone*"—the name the author operated with from 1995 until 2005, mainly lending it to "Druidic" publications, such as the *Draconomicon*, prior to developing his current "Mardukite Research Organization."

My interactions with Joshua Free—then "*Merlyn Stone*"—began long-distance via the internet shortly after an early copy of the *Draconomicon* crossed my path in 1997. The booklet was frugal and minimalist but inspired—a few dozen pages stapled together out of devotion by a thirteen-year old initiate of the modern "Pheryllt Druid" path, a subject of great controversy to neodruids at the time, but of even greater interest to me. And I was a bit baffled—here was a *kid* not only able to deliver his work—his very first work—somehow to my hands halfway across the globe (in a time well before internet media evolved to the social networking standard experienced today), yet all the more amazing to me was that he was somehow personally connected to the "Pheryllt" tradition suggested by controversial authors like Douglas Monroe and the New Forest group that I never seemed able to reach myself. Clearly this was a person that I needed to keep within my field of attentions, and I have for over two decades—without disappointment.

The real disappointment, since we have approached the topic, specifically regards the controversy and politics that overrun the potential tranquility of "neodruidism"—particularly the "Pheryllt" matter—something the author does not flee from in his writings. But, this is to be expected by someone that many consider the NexGen "darling" poster-child and spokesman of the neo-Pheryllt tradition—and a direct apprentice of Douglas Monroe. But, the two authors, while sharing many points and keystones of a paradigm, are very much individuals in their work and research—yet there is something very complimentary about their combination. The only point of contention put forth by Joshua Free to his mentor actually begins with the resulting intellectual conclusion of the *Draconomicon* research —what its author then spent 1998 until 2008 developing prior to his modern "Mardukite" inception, specifically: that *origins of Druidry lie in the Ancient Near East.*

This is no small point of fact for Joshua Free—it was a "theory" that set the author apart from nearly all other resources at my disposal, and he was firmly set in his resolve in this regard for his entire life, convinced of it from the time of his youth while compiling notebooks kept as a student and researcher of the *Pheryllt Druid* tradition—notebooks that developed into works of a *"young prodigious Merlyn Stone,"* carrying innovative and insightful "New Thought" all over the planet—and with some *drive*; this kid *really* wanted to be heard. Intrepidly doing so, he perhaps too often left himself wide open to the attack and ridicule of the then still up-and-coming Millennial "New Age" movement—one that was even less forgiving and more political than what we see on the internet today, if you can imagine.

On the surface and with little thought, it is easy to dismiss the author's "theories" as contradictory to all that we have come to know about the *History of the Druids*—and yet, what did we really know? Is it more difficult to speculate that the earliest "Druidic" *magi* emigrated from Mesopotamia—as did most all aspects tied to human civilization—rather than a mysterious island called *Atlantis* by the Greeks, lore Plato even borrowed heavily from the Egyptians and Mesopotamians, cultures that geographically appear quite distant from the Atlantic Ocean. This is not to say that there are not even more remote prehistoric factors contributing to the evolutionary continuum of human development, but even assuming that to be the case, Joshua Free suggests the *Ancient Near East* as the missing link bridging "prehistory" with known and popularized systems.

This has not made the author very popular...not in academic circles...not in New Age circles...leaving me with little wonder why he has so frequently culled together *his own* circles, forming *his own* underground "secret cabals" to work and operate freely—as per his name—uninhibited and without the scrutiny and closed-minded traditionalist rehash fundamentalism that appears to have set in as a "mainstream New Age" movement. This leaves Joshua Free and his *Pheryllt Druidism*, his "NexGen Systemology" and his "Mardukite" brand of (dare we call it) "Mesopotamian Neopaganism" all deeply recessed in a niche within a niche within a niche—written by an undeniably discarded gem and overlooked "misfit among misfit toys" that most people will never have the privilege of knowing during their lifetime—or his.

More to the point—although relayed with a casual coy sense of Millennial savvy and youthful "know-it-all*ness*," the intuited conclusions Joshua Free has drawn effortlessly throughout his numerous volumes of literary contribution all seem to make more sense the longer they are explored and the more personal research a *"seeker"* dedicates themselves to in verifying the facts that are actually buried beneath the surface of a world that we materially and intellectually take for granted.

The *Draconomicon* has been revised several times over the span of twenty-five years. Additions were incorporated each time to include the applicable research array for that period of the author's life. This continued up until five or so years ago when something truly unexpected happened: his original collection of *Pheryllt* research and development notebooks were revisited for an underground literary series—Joshua Free's recension of the *"Book of Pheryllt,"* first introduced in three installments, then published in its entirety as *"The Book of Pheryllt: A Complete Druid Source Book"* from Kima Global Books in 2018—the same publishers of the final installment of Douglas Monroe's Merlyn Trilogy, *"Deepteachings of Merlyn."* This makes *"Draconomicon"* the direct precursor for these other later releases by the author, nostalgically valuable in that right alone. And it is for this body of work that our paths again crossed.

Nearly ten years ago, during the initial development of Joshua Free's more widely known work pertaining to *Anunnaki* and *Babylon,* he approached me with an early copy of his book that described the *Dragon Legacy* using druidic, "elven" or "faerie" semantics, something later contributing directly to the early inception of the "Mardukite" paradigm—and yet I was immediately reminded of the main tenets of his *Draconomicon* all of those years earlier. After the author fell silent in 2001, I was left to wonder if we had heard all we were going to from him after all. Little did I know that all of that time (up until his reemergence from the shadows in 2008) he was quietly building up an inertia like a coil waiting to spring—and the vast array of intensive work delivered over the past decade is sure evidence that he has indeed *sprung.* In between all of this, I had one key contribution to make—and in gratitude for which the author granted me this opportunity to introduce his book.

There is a reoccurring appearance of a "Dragon magick" incantation referred to often as the *Welsh Charm of Making.* Yes, it *is* found frequently in magical rites associated with Douglas Monroe's *Pheryllt Druidism*—but, it *is* also found in many other sources, with recommendations for usage by numerous occult or esoteric authors, including papers from a "Merlin Temple" of the Hermetic Order of the Golden Dawn in England, documented for posterity in annals collected by Alan Richardson for his *"Ancient Magicks for a New Age."* The most famous pop-culture usage of the *Charm* is the 80's movie: *Excalibur* and as a result, revived amidst references used for the recent motion picture version of *Ready-Player One.* Douglas Monroe suggests an excerpt from one of the numerous volumes developed by the esoteric archaeologist Lewis Spence, where he writes:—

"Even some of the old Druidical cabbalistic expressions used in evoking, or calling up, the spirit of divination, still exist; for instance:
> *'anail nathrock uthvass*
> *bethudd, dochiel dienve'*
These words seem to be a sort of barbarous Irish form of an ancient Celtic expression, and are among the oldest surviving fragments of prehistoric verse to be recovered from Ogham inscriptions."

In his anthology, *"Book of Pheryllt,"* Joshua Free explains:—

"The *Charm* is usually written phonetically (seen above), a puzzle that made literal translation exceptionally difficult in 2008, when a member of the 'Mardukite Research Organization' worked it out..."

Almost needless to say, I *was* that "member." And I do believe it was around 2008, when Joshua Free was preparing his book *"Arcanum"* that I was approached to assist the matter of translation. He believed it *did* mean something—contrary to what every other "mainstream neodruid authority" professed. He explained to me that he knew that the first words had to mean "dragon's breath" but was unable to come to any further conclusions with his admittedly "slight" exploration into the old Celtic languages. I was familiar with the *Charm* from its previous references—but had never given it much thought. As with his other topics of controversy, he turned out to be *correct.*

Unlike other Indo-European languages, the old Celtic language group is exceptionally unique. There are some traditions that once considered *Gaelic* a "divine" or "angelic" language. And there are a wide array of derivative local languages that once spread throughout the United Kingdom, Scotland and Ireland, each observed in seeming isolation although geographically in quite close proximity to each other. Many old languages grow exceedingly more obscure every day due to shrinking usage. It is not so surprising that members of the western world might simply overlook "barbarous incantations" as nonsense.

I considered that the *Charm of Making* just might be written in some kind of "phonetic" attempt to capture the "sounds" of the words—as some of you familiar with Celtic languages will notice, many of the words are not spelled in a manner akin to how they sound when spoken. If that did not present enough of a challenge in itself, I was forced to consider—in spite of the *Gaelic* word for "breath" or "wind" used in *Welsh*, "anail"—that in light of the passage provided by Lewis Spence, if the *Charm* was actually a form of "*barbarous Irish*" then it wasn't *Welsh*.

Were it not for Joshua Free's insistence, I would never have done this work—and it wasn't so much a matter of being hard or difficult of a task, but one that I, in part, thought was a bit ridiculous at the start. Folks had used the *Charm of Making* off hand, tongue-in-cheek, for over a decade already—yet, at the same time, he had reminded me to another point-in-fact: that the incantation or evocation suggested by Douglas Monroe to connect with a spirit or "shade" of "Merlyn-the-Druid," came from a very real manuscript of *Welsh Archaeology*, called "The Stanzas of the Graves," which even included a *Gaelic* inscription presumably from the grave of the historical "Merlyn" (or "Merlin" if you prefer).

Clearly these specific names and incantations very selectively chosen to represent modern spiritual or metaphysical experiments *are* significant links connecting back to true ancient Druidic archetypes and raw energies of true ancient magic.

Since the translation did not appear in former editions of the *Draconomicon*, it would seem fitting and most appropriate to share that here, at the 25th Anniversary threshold of *seekers* entering the threshold of a "dragon mystery tradition" within its pages.

THE PHERYLLT/DRAGON "CHARM OF MAKING"

Dragon's Breath
Spell of Life and Death
Thy Charm of Making

anail nathair (*anail nathrack*)
"breath"/"wind" — "serpent"/"dragon"

orth'bhais's bethad (*ortha bhais-is beatha*)
"spell" — "life" — "death"

do cheal deanaimh (*do chel denmha*)
"thy" — "charm" — "making"

Now that we have put the controversial subject of the *Charm of Making* to rest, the second matter to resolve, perhaps even more controversial, regards the reoccurring theme present in most *"Druidic writings"* by Joshua Free regarding the origins of the Pheryllt and/or Druids in Mesopotamia. This theme is sure to catch many folk off guard and has been a constant source of contention between the author and many of his harsher critics and less informed readers. There is little doubt that it is a shocking or surprising conclusion expressed by the author for at least two decades—but the author has remained steadfast, again, in their resolve that their "intuitions" were right. This pursuit became such an occupation for the author that he spent most of this current millennium attempting to establish this point to esoteric audiences...with mixed results.

One theory put forth by Joshua Free, keystone to his writings, regards a prehistoric collective migration of Mesopotamian systemology across Europe, citing examples of the *La Tene* culture and marked by the indigenous traditions developed later in vicinity to the Danube River, one of two pathways he suggested that it probably traveled. He states that it is only the result of Roman intervention and the domination of the "Classical World" over the former ancient one that pushed these traditions and evidence for them into specific concentrated locations—such as we easily can see with the "Celtic World" that is traditionally attributed exclusively to the British Isles or Ireland, yet it once served as a dominating influence for most of the European continent. How easily we forget... One additional facet of this theory is that prior to the migration, a localized concentration of this population emerged from the *Ancient Near East* and gathered in ancient *Anatolia*—the place of the legendary "Drunemeton," a secret birthplace of Druidry that only the highest ranks among them knew of and would regularly return to during their lifetimes. All wild theories?

In April 2019, the BBC headlines read: "DNA Reveals Origins of Stonehenge Builders." Articles provided research summaries published in *Nature, Ecology & Evolution*. It described a neolithic western migration in c. 6000 B.C. from *Anatolia*, modern-day Turkey, across two routes—the Mediterranean and Danube River Valley—which spread early Mesopotamian knowledge of agriculture across Europe, reaching Britain by c. 4000 B.C...

I've decided to take the writings by Joshua Free *even more* seriously. I would encourage anyone else to perhaps do the same.

Wishing you the best, from the arms of the Dragon.

—Rowen Gardner
Summer 2019
Wales, U.K.

INTRODUCTION TO THE DRACONOMICON
25TH ANNIVERSARY

by Joshua Free

Twenty-five years have now passed since I first became active in modern *Pheryllt Druidism*. My debut publication known as the *Draconomicon* first emerged out of a research notebook I kept from that period—during a time of investigation into all matters related to the "*Dragon*." Although the purpose and spirit of the work remains unchanged, the literal text has seen revision, alteration and enhancement *four* times prior to reaching its current state—marking a legacy of underground influence for neo-Druidic (and other) movements for now a quarter-of-a-century in this "New Age."

It is no secret that the *Draconomicon* represents the forerunner of my original vision for a personal "*Book of Pheryllt*" or "books of *Fferyllt*," an intellectual and spiritual collection of lore also called the "*Body of the Dragon*." The ancient "Druid Order" of the Celts dedicated themselves to preservation of this lore, at least among their own elite sect of educated "learned ones." It may be covertly found throughout surviving Bardic remnants of Celtic cosmology, spirituality, natural and native histories, medicinal and botanical knowledge, not to mention celestial knowledge of astronomy and the esoteric arts of "magic."

The subject of the *Dragon* is *universal*—infused within and encompassing the whole of the *cosmos*. This same universe or cosmos—the ordered material existence we experience every day—is represented by a *Dragon* in all of the most ancient accounts, as are the "microcosmic" levels of the same reality, the fragmentation of the "*dragon-mind*" or "universal consciousness" into separate parts, whether these *Dragons* are literally realized as spiritual, religious, cosmological, biological, or even completely immaterial symbols enshrouded in more occult esoterica than is worth deciphering. But inseparable from this path of discovery—is the *Dragon*.

Since my youth, the *Dragon* remained always something of a secret passion for me. Having initially been raised to a Catholic standard, I was surrounded by indoctrination to believe that all *"dragons"* related back to something "of the devil." And while I did not especially adopt that paradigm, it did affect the way I could express my interests. This, of course, all changed in 1995, when I first immersed myself with the *Dragon Path* and found myself working with a small Pheryllt study group in Minneapolis, called the "Mystics of the Earth" and armed with little more than Douglas Monroe's *"21 Lessons of Merlyn."*

The next year, during high school, I relocated to the Colorado Rocky Mountains and carried the spirit and leadership of the former disbanded group with me, starting the "Draconis Celtic Lodge of Druids" (later evolving into the "Elven Fellowship Circle of Magick") in Denver. I accomplished this at fourteen years old, simultaneously the youngest initiate of the "Order of Bards, Ovates & Druids" in England and working at a distance with Douglas Monroe and his "New Forest Centre for Magickal Studies." When the former discovered the latter, I was immediately unseated from OBOD membership and classified alongside Monroe as "heretical neodruidism." But—some things are just *meant to be.*

This turn of events allowed me to focus more closely on my own work. The new group was still rooted deeply in *Pheryllt Druidism*, but by that time I had already started to incorporate Mesopotamian elements as an extension of the *Dragon Mystery Tradition*, particularly the Marduk-and-Tiamat motif present in the Babylonian *"Epic of Creation,"* the oldest written *genesis* account on the planet. As many might suspect, this shift in emphasis later evolved into my current more widely visible "Mardukite" pursuits, including a presentation of such under a guise respectfully advancing the quasi-Babylonian Anunnaki paradigm alluded to in the famous *Simon Necronomicon.*

The original *Draconomicon* that I released underground in 1996 (subtitled: *Secrets of Sanguis Draconis*) was honestly more like a fanciful "pamphlet" than the actual "book" it later evolved to. It summarized a minimalist background in "dragon lore," but also suggested roots for my theories that connected ancient (or prehistoric) Druidism with the Mesopotamian paradigms—both seeming to share an emerging influence all over the planet as if from nowhere, if we cling to accepted theories.

After careful consideration, we cannot dismiss the far sweeping influence of the genuine *Dragon Legacy* in human systems and on human consciousness. Evidence for it may be found at the heart of virtually every ancient systemology, pantheons or spiritual system—regardless of how clearly or *Self-honestly* it is met with by seekers. We can also not dismiss more obvious effects on mass consciousness resulting from thousands of years of "*demonization of the Dragon*" by the Western World—further even, the dualistic and polarized dogmas of "good-versus-evil" paramount to the existence of all our most popular systems alive today: Judaic, Christian, Islamic, Zoroastrian, &tc.

In ancient esoteric lore, the *Dragon* appears in cosmological accounts describing formation and ordering of the *cosmos*, itself a *Cosmic Dragon* born from the primordial Abyss. On a human biological level, the *Dragon* illustrates the serpent-coil of DNA—the genetic memory and conditional potential that is wound up within each of us, waiting to be unfolded by our ascent up the "ladder of ascension" on the *Dragon Path*. Even among esoteric representatives of underground occult mysteries that are shielded from the eyes and ears of the surface world, we see and hear the invocations and calls to the *Dragon* ring out loudly from those who seek to understand the "*Truth Against the World*" and a *Self-honest* participation with Reality.

It is a joy, after so many years, to see a newer, expanded and greatly improved version of the *Draconomicon* that exceeds the abilities I possessed as a researcher and publisher a quarter-of-a-century ago. The world is also a different place—far and removed from New Age peaks and breakthroughs taking place in the mid-1990's when the "underground" became public.

We suddenly saw a huge revival in "magickal" interests swell from its incline in the 1970's and 1980's as the "New Age marketplace" first formed. Suddenly these obscure oddities once reserved to dark alleys and dank fens now started to grace the shopping centers and local malls. More titles were flooding into "New Age" and "supernatural/paranormal" genres than ever before. Publishers were quick to find anyone that would lend their personal *spellbooks* and *Books of Shadows* to the market. Suddenly being in a "coven" was fashionable, and we were overrun with a significant amount of repetitive "neopagan" materials all validating each other within hermetically sealed confines of this new "movement." Most of these fell by the wayside; a few became underground cult classics—but in my opinion, little advancement has since been made in the mainstream/contemporary New Age approaches, and in fact, most newer rehashes have become quite diluted when compared to their former source texts.

While the mainstream has remained mostly fixed on neopagan ideologies that often revive any or all aspects of ancient pantheism and cultural mythologies arbitrarily—we have seen an increase in progressive activity in the underground, also publicly visible during the new millennium, particularly related to the rising use of the *internet* and especially the "Web 2.0" that quickly resulted, far more interactive and focused on social networking than the static internet of the 1990's. While it did open up many "underground" elements and facets of lore to the public, it also greatly enabled those of us already working in the underground to develop covert networks and alliances as a reaction—or perhaps antidote—to rapid world changes. Sometimes these alliances grew less covert over time, particularly in regard to "independent publishing," which is the only surface-world industry that actively feeds our type of work. It hits those of us who have had much to say, but for whatever the reasons, have been slighted out by the "big game" players and are usually forced to remain in the underground supported by small followings. And it is not a matter of merit. There is a lot of politics at play—even in an "enlightening New Age."

Draconomicon is special to me for a myriad of reasons. Yes, it is true that it was my debut writings, but it also set the precedent for my later literary work, which in turn served as my gateway into greater underground networks. By this, I am referring to the total cycle of material dubbed "Liber-D" in the "Mardukite" research catalogue, of which *Draconomicon* is an integral part and the original launch point. Not only did it contribute to my later collected anthology *"Book of Pheryllt,"* but it served as an inspiration to pursue my own quest to uncover the *Dragon Legacy* on earth—something I also brought to another part of the "Liber-D" cycle, released underground as *"Book of Elven-Faerie,"* which was a trilogy of materials in itself. Shortly thereafter, I compiled the *"Arcanum"* and that began a whole new chapter of life with the *"Mardukites"* ...and the rest, as they say, is history.

Now that you've received all of the background, there is only one remaining pleasantry for me to impart—

May you have safe passage through Dragon Country!

—Joshua Free
Summer 2019
Colorado, USA

DRACONOMICON

HISTORY, MAGIC & TRADITIONS
of DRAGONS, DRUIDS and
THE PHERYLLT

DRAGONS OF SUMERIA
—MESOPOTAMIA—

The true *Dragon Legacy* extends throughout time and space without inhibition, and for whatever it has come to later encompass to the initiated, or represent to commoners, it has a definitive origin on planet earth—one that can be found in ancient *Mesopotamia*. To understand this fully in all of its wide-angle glory requires a knowledge base extending beyond the direct emphasis of this current work. Much is carefully documented throughout collected literary works delivered from the "Mardukite Research Organization." Therefore, it is not the purpose of this text to simply "rehash" an entire body of publications—rather it is the intention to shine a new light of unification regarding the *Dragon*—a vast topic that touches on, or overlaps, many other subjects and themes that are fundamental to numerous mystical and magical pursuits today, just as they were in the days of the Ancient Mystery School.

Extending our mind to the most discrete past—based on currently available esoteric knowledge—we are confronted with a colorful world of primordial and primeval monsters. Many are beyond comprehension of modern humans, those with no direct overt encounters to mirror the very real images registered in genetic memory. For many people, the matter of the *Dragon* is ridiculous fantasy, with no literal connection to any "monstrous" creations on this planet—or throughout the cosmos.

If we turn toward physical archaeology for our answers, there is little direct evidence to counter "skeptics" believing that the *Dragon*—as a "biological entity"—is purely the product of imagination. Perhaps paleontology would provide more clues, if we consider dinosaurs, although these creatures supposedly exist only in the relatively distant "geologic" past, that should otherwise, according to contemporary historians, have no "overlap" of occurrence with the existence of modern "*homo sapien sapien*"—humans. Other than obscure fossil records, the only place a seeker is able to turn for advice remain the oldest written records on the planet, drawn from the literal birthplace of modern writing—which is to say, Mesopotamia.

The beauty of using the Mesopotamian paradigm as a "Source-tradition" or "baseline" is that it is not only historically logical to do so, given its place in history, but the material it offers is a far more "complete" and comprehensible rendering of the ancient world than what was preserved from memory across time and space by various cultures, each adapting inherited knowledge to fit their own unique needs. Mesopotamian records include allusions to "monstrous creations" throughout the cosmos that precede the existence of humanity altogether. Maybe the nature of *dinosaurs* is not so clearly understood. It also begs the question of genetic engineering and "third-party manipulation" taking place not only on earth, but in other "worlds" as well. To the esoterically uneducated (uninitiated) minds, such concepts are seemingly unfathomable!

Let us consider for a moment, outside a purely Celto-European geography and semantics, prior to use in human traditions (and other programmed systems of civilization), both spiritual and political (or worldly), the most fundamental and ancient lore of the *Dragon* comes to us by way of—and as interconnected to—beings known and recorded on ancient Mesopotamian cuneiform tablets as the "*Anunnaki.*" I would refer a perceptive student to a most fundamentally paramount series among the post-Sumerian—Mardukite Babylonian—accounts of the *Epic of Creation*, those which have been often misunderstood as "Sumerian," what scholars notably call the "Enuma Eliš" (or "Emuma Elish")—a series of seven (six plus one) cuneiform tablets forged by the "Nabu Priesthood" in Babylon as a means of elevating the status of MARDUK, an Anunnaki Prince-Son of ENKI (the brother of ENLIL).

These *Draconomicon* notebooks are at first dedicated to the spirit of the ancient *Pheryllt*, the "first systematizers of the Celts" originating in prehistoric times and working their way through the valleys of Europe before reaching the homestead in the Welsh mountains where they are most famously recognized—for upon which the Oxford universities coincidentally now are located. But these are dedicated equally to that spirit in all of its integrity—*the Truth against the World*—and pursuits to discover the underlying origins, information that does not appear to be in consensus with my contemporaries, many of which do not feel, as I do, the connection between Druidism and Mesopotamia. As the *Draconomicon* notebooks are also a part of a specifically "Druidic cycle" of literature, it is not my intention to rehash volumes of background material regarding the "Mardukite Babylonian" paradigm, information that may be easily gleaned from my other works. But—there *is* an overlap, a synchronous interconnectivity, and as such we may have to reiterate some of the main tenets here, aspects of the tradition that can be illustrated within the present theme.

Opening lines of the Enuma Eliš—as relayed in *"The Complete Anunnaki Bible"** Mardukite Tablet-N* series—are as follows:

When in the heights the Heavens
Had not been named,
And the Earth had not yet been named,
And the Primeval APSU [Abyss], who birthed them,
And TIAMAT—
The Ancient One—Mother to them ALL.

What we are given here is a description of the formation (or formulation) of the universe as a material matrix-structure. The "ordering" of the "infinite" as the cosmos, else the Cosmic Dragon. From out of Nothingness is the Abyss—and from the Abyss was spawned (fragmented) the first of the material creatures, TIAMAT, the primeval dragon and "Mother" to ALL.

---

* Alternatively released as *"Necronomicon: The Anunnaki Bible"* hardcover and abridged pocket-paperback editions by Joshua Free.

Later, from the same tablet, we are given a description of *her* ability to further "spawn" (fragment) material existence into "monstrous" and "horrific" creations that now seem to only imaginatively plague men in their nightmares.

> TIAMAT spawned monster-serpents,
> Sharp of tooth and merciless of fang;
> With poison, instead of blood,
> She filled their bodies.
> Fierce monster-vipers she clothed with terror.
> She set up vipers and dragons,
> And the monster LAHAMU...
> After this fashion,
> She made eleven kinds of monsters.

Notice that we say *her* and the authors say *mother*. Clearly, in most interpretations of the Mesopotamian Mythos, the being identified as TIAMAT (or sometimes transliterated, TI.AM.TU) is depicted very specifically as a *Female Dragon*. She is spawned from the Abyss—as the first movement or *primum mobile*—and given admiration in the most ancient accounts as the *Mother-Matrix* responsible for all later forms of life and existence (as an archetypal "first-form" herself). Noticeably, in these later "Babylonian" accounts—such as the historians are most likely to rely on—the actual politics and purpose of the narrative is overlooked. It is disguised within the text, so it is not so surprising that only some select esoteric researchers understand.

The codex preserved in the Babylonian "Epic of Creation" is incorporated into Mardukite *systemology* and therein receives its value in the ancient world far more than any of its cosmogenetic qualities. It is set in a time before "earth" or "men," describing primordial events that led to fragmented ordering. It is quite possible that "*demonization of the Dragon*" was not at first an invention of the "Church." Rather, we find evidence in Babylonian spiritual politics, which did not so much "demonize" all depictions of the "dragon" as evil, but instead showed that dominance over it represented "cosmic authority."

In the *"Enuma Eliš"* we are given a political account of *Marduk* slaying the "Cosmic Serpent"—or *Dragon*—representing his prowess in "overcoming chaos" in the universe to establish his own *"cosmos"* or "World Order." In part, this was actually an older "Sumerian" concept concerning *Kur*, the "Dragon of the Mountain" from a pre-Babylonian Mesopotamian mythos. But, in Babylon, this "Ancient Dragon" represented an "Old Way" that had to be overturned in order to raise a new one— the "Mardukite" Anunnaki paradigm in Babylon, dedicated in political and spiritual reverence to Marduk. By performing this cosmic dragon-slaying feat and thereby ordering or re-ordering the cosmos, Marduk is recognized as "King of the Anunnaki" in Babylonian "Mardukite" lore. Yes, performing this amazing feat, even if only symbolically or as an archetype in global consciousness, these "Mardukite" forces represented in Babylon are given the "Divine Right" to exercise all Anunnaki powers on Earth... and, on earth, as it is in heaven...

While not directly inferred from more widely known versions of the Enuma Eliš, some interpretations have identified Marduk as not only a *"dragon-god,"* but a direct descendent of the Cosmic Dragon, TIAMAT. In fact, many surface world "schoolhouse" lessons of the "Epic of Creation" describe Marduk as a son of TIAMAT. But perhaps the most historical, political and spiritual shortcoming to outsider (uninitiated) exploration of the *"Enuma Eliš"* is the fact of its blatant misrepresentation as a "Sumerian" treatise, when it is all-at-once "Babylonian."

Marduk, the chief of the Anunnaki pantheon in Babylon, does not make any appearance in all of the loosely systematized pre-Babylonian "Sumerian Religions." This more antiquated *Enlilite* observation of the "Old Ways" (by Babylonian standards) seemed to improperly evolve with the complex rise of human systems, and acknowledged only primitive traditions of *Enlil*, brother to *Enki*. In order to raise Marduk to a height of power in Babylon, the focal shift of universal order necessarily had to be replaced, meaning a paradigm elevating *Marduk* via *Enki*, thus overshadowing the former "Sumerian" worldview.

If we treat the discourse chronologically as literal references to actual living beings, for example—the Anunnaki—then it would seem that the "Epic" is either allegorical or referring to a separate incident altogether. Some historians and biblical scholars have postulated that it is a *cosmological treatise* that describes the formation of the local universe and the activity of celestial bodies—such as planets—that share names with those Anunnaki figures popularized by Mesopotamian mythology. For example, Marduk replaces Enlil as "Jupiter" after the local "solar system" is formed. During this formation, however, there is a cataclysmic event involving either "Jupiter" or some other "Celestial body"—else one of its moons. In effect, we are given the field of local space known as the "asteroid belt" that resulted from a primordial event. It is postulated further that the local Earth-moon system and the ability to culminate intelligent life here were also consequences to this event. Should that all be the case, then the "Epic" is sound in the literal *cosmogenetic* respects. But, that is not the way in which the materials were used in ordering and systematizing ancient Mesopotamia. Because we know now that Marduk, a member of a "Younger Generation" Anunnaki, would not necessarily have been present during "cosmic formation." What is described on the tablets must therefore have held both a public *exoteric* meaning among the masses in addition to the more intellectually guarded *esoteric* meaning maintained by the select few properly "initiated" to behold the mysteries.

True, there are a few pre-Babylonian "Sumerian" tablets with very loose references to deities slaying an ancient dragon named KUR—but these are later rendered insignificant when compared to the greater paradigm of Mesopotamian systems. Once the Babylonian shift takes place, a connection between Earthly kingship ("*Enlilship*") and the *Dragon* becomes fundamentally inseparable. Then, when we consider the possible existence of the *Sirrush* "Dragon of Babylon," such as is visually depicted on the walls and art of the city, this iconic image of the *Dragon* further led Babylonian consciousness toward accepting Marduk as *Supreme Dragonmaster—King of the Gods.*

Tablet VI of the Enuma Eliš—as relayed in *"The Complete Anunnaki Bible"** Mardukite Tablet-N*—describes a lengthy, brutal and horrific battle between TIAMAT and Marduk before he proves successful in slaying the beast. What follows thereafter may be interpreted as the formation/separation of heaven and earth:

> Gazing upon the dead body of TIAMAT,
> MARDUK devised a cunning plan.
> He split her up into two halves;
> One half of her he established a veil for heaven.
> He sealed it with a "GATE"
> And he stationed a watcher—IAK SAKKAK,
> And fixed him
> Not to let her waters ever come forth.

Prior to Babylonian systematization, the Sumerian worldview held a more primitive cosmological model in mass awareness, describing a division of the heaven and earth zones decided by the "Way of ANU," the paternal Anunnaki "King of the Gods" and father of Enlil and Enki. The "Way of ANU" included his decree that he would remain the distant and fatherly "God" in the starry heavens, leaving the two brothers to maintain "material control." In doing so, Enlil became the "Lord of the Airy Space" and Enki controlled the "Firmament of Earth." Although the primary division of heaven and earth was wholly fixed, solidified and concrete, this still left many aspects of a "space" and "earth" systemology to be debated. The "Order" decreed by Anu was never questioned in Enlilite-dominated Sumerian Religion, but with the rise of Marduk and Babylon, this changed, and the icon of its change: *The Dragon.*

Today, in the NexGen field of Esoteric Archaeology, we now recognize this description of dragonslaying that appears in the Enuma Eliš as the first piece of literary propaganda to develop in human history. As it was not literal, no ethical issue existed about the moral nature of "Dragons" that were never killed.

---

*   Alternatively released as *"Necronomicon: The Anunnaki Bible"* hardcover and abridged pocket-paperback editions by Joshua Free.

Original cuneiform tablet authors—a society of priest-scribes working very closely with Babylonian systematization, and dedicated to the god Nabu, herald and heir of Marduk—used the iconic imagery of dragons to impact global perceptions of not only the identity of the Anunnaki themselves, but also as a symbolic representation of their "worldly authority." Human populations continued to grow and feed this systematization of life, so long as its structure properly met their physical needs. Ancient sages structured these pagan source traditions first and foremost to maintain the annual agricultural cycle, and populations flourished once communities understood the way in which sustainable foodstuffs could be grown. For this reason, many of the most antiquated deities and esoteric systems emphasize agriculture, fertility, water and pasturing. It is only later, after these primitive needs were met, that Babylonian religion grew in complexity toward a reverence to gods of wisdom, knowledge, justice, law, &tc.

In Babylon, the Dragon became a national icon of the city, its cultural power and its patron Anunnaki deities, Marduk and Nabu. Surviving records are obscure, but it seems that at one juncture the Babylonian Kings and Temple precinct once was in possession of actual living beasts resembling the Dragon depicted in Babylonian art—the Sirruš or Sirrush, from which we may also derive the name Sirius. According to available lore, of Marduk's two half-brothers—Ningishzida (or Ninrah) and Ninazu (or Tišpak)—this Dragon was first a creature kept by Ninazu, but it was gifted to Marduk during his ascent up the Mesopotamian pantheon in Babylon. As the royal family pet, the secrets of the SIRRUSH came into Nabu's possession, and it is theorized that these magnificent otherworldly beasts were kept by true Kings of Babylon up until the time of Nabuchadnezzar—perhaps the last of the great Babylonian kings.

The traditional name of the Dragon of Babylon—Sirruš—is also equated to the Akkadian-language name for a dragon species called the *mushhushshu* or *mušuššu*, meaning "ferocious serpent," from the root *mushus* (mušus) or "monster." This is not the same species-type as TIAMAT—an *usumgal*, or "Great Cosmic Serpent"—which represents the whole local universe.

Interestingly, far away in the African Congo, a description of the *mushushu* matches a species of *sauropod*—now believed to be extinct—called *mokele-mbembe* by indigenous tribes that claimed to have killed one. If so, this could effectively connect dragon-lore with saurians (dinosaurs). And yet, where *Dragon lore* appears universal on planet earth, contemporary knowledge of "dinosaurs" is only present in public consciousness for the past 200 years.

The subject of this *Dragon* is raised in Willy Ley's underground classic "Exotic Zoology," which dedicates an entire chapter to *'The Sirrush of the Ishtar Gate'*—opening with:

> "When on June 3, 1887, Professor Robert Koldewey of Germany, on a hurried two-day visit to the site of ancient Babylon, picked up a fragment of old brick, one surface of which was covered with a bright blue glaze, he probably expected to make an archaeological discovery, but he did not dream how big a discovery it would turn out to be. And he certainly did not imagine that it would pose a zoological puzzle which is still as provocative today as it was a half-century ago."

Later on he describes:

> "The Ishtar Gate is an enormous semicircular arch flanked by gigantic walls and opening toward a procession way of considerable length, which is also flanked right and left by walls. The building material is brick, glazed bright blue, yellow, white, and black. To increase the splendor, the walls of the gate and the processional way [street] are covered with bas-reliefs of unusual beauty, showing animals in very lifelike positions."

The specific animal of current significance:

"...is commonly referred to as the Dragon of Babylon and it is the same "animal" that is mentioned by that name in the Bible. The Babylonian name for it has been preserved in cuneiform inscriptions, but there is some doubt as to the correct pronunciation. At first the sign (it denotes the plural of the word) was read *sir-ruššu*; the name would, therefore be *sirrush*. But it has also been read *muš-ruššû* (*mushrush*) and translated loosely into the German as *Prachtschlange*. This could be loosely rendered in English as "Splendor Serpent" or "Glamour Snake." However, until one of those terms is more widely accepted, it is better to use *sirrush*, which is the term Koldewey preferred."

In order to more accurately understand the tremendous impression the *Dragon* left on public consciousness via its appearance on Babylonian infrastructure—including the design and artistic renderings for its gates and walls—we turn to Robert Koldewey's own words:

"The rows are repeated one above the other; dragons and bulls are never mixed in the same horizontal row, but a line of bulls is followed by one of *sirrush*. Each single representation of an animal occupies a height of 13 brick courses, and between them are 11 plain courses, so that the distance from the foot of one to the foot of the next is 24 courses. These 24 courses together measure almost exactly two meters (6 feet, 8 inches) or four Babylonian *ells* in height.

"Originally there were thirteen rows of animals, beginning with a top row of *sirrush*; each of the eight lower rows contained at least forty animals and each of the five upper rows at least fifty-one, so that the grand total of animal pictures on the gate amounts to about 575. It is certainly an impressive structure, and it is not at all surprising that King Nebuchadnezzar, who was responsible for reconstructing the Ishtar Gate, was very proud of it. When it was finished he composed an inscription—written down in cuneiform characters for all to read. With a lack of modesty then customary it began:

'Nabu-ku-dur-ri-u-su-ur [Nebuchadnezzar], the King of Babylon, the pious Prince, ruling by the will and grace of Marduk [the supreme god of the Babylonians], supreme ruler of the City, beloved by Nebo* [son of Marduk, supreme god of the neighboring city of Borsippa], of clever cunning, who never tires . . . and ever works for the welfare of Babylon, the wise one—I am the first-born son of Nabopolassar, King of Babylon. Fierce bulls [the original says *rimi*] and grim dragons I put onto the gate-yard [meaning its walls] and thus supplied the gates with such overflowing rich splendor that all humanity may view it with wonderment.'"

Elsewhere in Willy Ley's discourse, he continues to comment on Babylonian zoological art:

"In ancient Greece, too, the Ishtar Gate was well known by name and reputation, but the name used was the 'Gate of Semiramis.' Of course no one of those who saw the Ishtar Gate in those days was plagued by zoological scruples. The lions on the walls of the procession way were lions, the bulls on the gate were bulls—even if they did look slightly unusual; and that King Nebuchadnezzar's artisans had seen fit to add a monster of their own invention did not trouble anyone. They had also occasionally pictured eagles with the heads of bearded men, and other hybrid monsters. In short, the pictures of the *sirrush* caused no astonishment. It required the tremendously enlarged knowledge of the later age that excavated and reconstructed the Ishtar Gate to feel astonishment about those peculiar pictures."

The actual description, he reiterates most eloquently:

---

* *Nebo*, alternately transliterated as *Nabu* in "Mardukite" literature.

"Bas-reliefs of *sirrush* are very definite in outline and show a slender body covered with scales, a long slender scaly tail, and a long slim scaly neck bearing a serpent's head. Although the mouth is closed, a long forked tongue protrudes. There are flaps of skin attached to the back of the head, which is adorned (and armed) with a straight horn—possibly a pair of horns, since the pictures of the *re'em* also show only one horn. Most remarkable, however, are the feet. The forefeet are those of a catlike animal, say a panther, but the hind feet are those of a bird. They are very large and four-toed, covered with strong scales. And in spite of the combination of so many different characteristics the *sirrush* looks tremendously alive, at least as much so as the *re'em* shown next to it, if not more so."

And finally, the logical connection to dinosaurs is made:

"If the Ishtar Gate had been excavated a century earlier, this combination of catlike forefeet and birdlike hind feet would have been sufficient proof that the "Glamour Snake" was no whit more credible than the winged bulls and man-headed birds of Assyrian and Babylonian mythology. During these hundred years, however, Georges Cuvier had become the 'Father of Paleontology,' Professor O. C. Marsh in America had earned the title of "Father of Dinosaurs," and our conceptions of what was biologically possible had changed greatly. Paleontologists had discovered fossil animals that sported incredibly long necks and tails, big bodies and small heads, serpent heads with horns on them (and possibly even forked tongues, although unfortunately tongues do not fossilize), and similar attributes. They had even found a type of dinosaurs that walked upright on their birdlike hind legs, waving smaller five-toed forelegs in the air."

The esoteric implications described throughout this chapter—and in effect the whole *Draconomicon* project—carry many advanced applications once we can learn the holistic secret of blending all true and faithful data into a wide-angle picture, thereby having an intellectual capacity to explore the full *systemology* of existence in magical practices, exercises of energy that have an ability to affect our everyday lives. Nothing in life is truly inconsequential—therefore the wizard's art is only fully accessible to one who operates a *Self-honest* experience of the world. Without this, we fall prey to the same fanciful pitfalls that render public New Age displays as "ridiculous."

Mesopotamian lore therefore offers us four—yes, *four!*—distinct concepts of the *Dragon*, most of which originate on the same tablet cycle:

(1) TIAMAT as *usumgal*, the "cosmic dragon"
(2) LAHAMU and other "dragon-monsters"
(3) MARDUK as an Anunnaki (*anu-nagi*) "star-dragon"
(4) SIRRUSH and other "animal-dragons"

With little surprise, the esoteric conception of the "universe" as a "Great Dragon" may be traced back to the most definitive example of this—found in the ancient Sumerian current of KUR, and Babylonian TIAMAT. In effect, a modern seeker of the true *Dragon* mysteries requires a certain degree of open-minded wide-angle approaches to appreciate everything this pursuit encompasses—everything from the most biologically tangible to the most spiritually immaterial elements.

The "secret" is really that these are all connected—All-as-One—that it is really the individualized pursuits and reality experience of mortals that makes them appear so distinct, abstract or else mutually exclusive possibilities.

Mystics, magicians and wizards have often relayed esoteric knowledge that the universe is a Dragon, but then we also find later implications that the planet earth is as like the body of a

Dragon, or that the energetic currents and lines of power on earth are pulsing veins of Dragon's blood... All of this we can attribute first to the prehistoric Dragons of Sumer and preservation of its knowledge in the cuneiform literary tradition of Mesopotamia in Babylon.

DRAGONS OF ThE DEEP
—EUROPEAN INFESTATION—

Strong tides of emotional and political impact swept through human consciousness from the inception of civilization and its foundation in the Babylonian "Epic of Creation." Raising Marduk (as *"Jupiter"*) to power in Babylon required the fragmentation of the "Universal Dragon" into the 'currents' or 'gates' that Marduk—and his chosen priests and kings—could govern as acting intermediaries between the human population and the "Divine," thereby controlling the reality affecting human experience of *Heaven and Earth* under the banner of the "Royal Dragon." Later appearances of the *Dragon* motif outside the domain of Mesopotamia came swiftly and sure.

To the "Pheryllt" Druids, the *Dragon* symbolized not only the "greater universe" and cosmic order existing seemingly apart from the immediately affecting physical world of earth-life, but also political and religious mastery of the same as represented on earth. This is best realized with the "charge" that the "Holy Church" was given at its inception that "on earth as it is in heaven," implying that what "chosen dragon rulers" decreed on "earth," would also be in "heaven"—suggesting its being "blessed by God" and enacted on "earth" by *Divine Right*. In essence, this is what has been meant by *dragon power* since the time of Babylon, including among proto-Druid founders—the *Pheryllt* Priesthood.

Whether represented by a cosmic spiritual entity, a biological form, or a reptilian humanoid, there are some very *key* "currents" or moves of energy that are connected to the *Dragon*. In and of itself, this should be suggestive to an inquisitive mind that there is *some kind* of unification behind it all.

The DRAGON represents:

> Order, Science, Intellect, Sovereignty,
> Ancientness, Primeval, Primordial, Esoteric,
> Secrets, Animal, Material, Reptile, Energy,
> Power, Stars, Strength, Will, Action,
> Information, Creation, Chaos.

Of course, examining the list alone will not necessarily bring the seeker to any great conclusions or mystical gnosis, but it will become readily apparent to most that this is what it is all about in this world, in spite of what we might wish or be expected to color it as.

The *Dragon* is depicted in the most ancient lore as representative of everything as one! It is both the primeval and undistinguished ocean of consciousness and chaos as well as the fragmented and pointedly manifest physical existence. It is the epitome of the most spiritual and intangible of abstract ideals in the cosmos as much as it is the definitive representation of the solid physics we most closely identify as "real."

Between the Earth and Sky (or Universe), both of which are in themselves referred to as the *dragon*, we find the "ambassadors" *between the worlds*—aliens, sky gods, kings, druids, &tc.— also referred to as *dragons*, or carrying *dragonblood* thereby linking them to the "legacy" genetically. By some abstract semantics, the "sacred knowledge" of the 'Great Work Mystery Tradition of the Ages' is called "star-knowledge" or "dragon-knowledge" not only because of its source, but as a result of its relay to the population: using "Divinely Ordained" *Dragon Kings, Priestesses, Priest-Scribes, bards* and *magicians*.

The current seeker is forced to make some decisions from this point on regarding exactly what perspective they are going to adopt when interpreting dragon references in not only this book, but throughout all lore available at their disposal. One can easily fall into the view typically held by the skeptics who discard the entire subject simply because they dislike the choice of vocabulary or semantics, thereby attacking any lore produced by "mythologists" as nothing more than superstitious beliefs about lightning, volcanoes or even supernovas. At the same time there is a portion of the population that is not comfortable accepting this reality consensus—the types that are generally more likely to pursue a work like *Draconomicon*.

Seekers are presented with the possibility of the Dragon as a biological entity, meaning for the earth planet: firstly the dinosaurs that emerged either "naturally" (according to some views of "terrestrial evolution") or by some form of *intervention* (either direct genetic experimentation or selective breeding). Secondly, we are given this idea of an "ancient alien" paradigm that forms a potential basis of what we dare to call "divine" by our distant ancestors—beings that themselves appear "reptilian," "draconian" or "draconial" in themselves, or at the very least are frequently represented by such. Finally, if we are to adopt any and all of the "ancient sky god" aspects to our reality of Dragon Lore, we cannot rule out possible physical and technological means by which they traveled and operated, which could also be denoted as dragon-like.

Mythologies surrounding the "Sky Gods" and *dragons* (regardless of the cultural pantheon or semantics adopted) have yet another *key* element involved that not only links them to each other, but also to the practices and beliefs that erupted as well: *mountains*.

It is the "mountaintops" and "high places" that seem to be of significant interest to the *dragon-like* "deities" themselves as well as those half-mortals and demi-gods who came to serve as their ambassadors. In the case of non-mountainous terrain without such geology, "artificial peaks" in the form of pyramidal structures were raised in their stead—and we should not be surprised that they are also sacred to these *dragon gods*. Using the historical and verifiable (and visible) sources of tradition, we can attribute a *dragon-energy* to the socio-poltical and religio-spiritual use of the mountains in relation to the later emerging "Sky God" traditions, including: pyramids, ziggurats, temples, burial mounds and other "artificial hillsides."

Mountains and *Dragons* have gone together since the time of the Sumerians and Babylonians in ancient Mesopotamia. In fact, the oldest name given on the pre-Babylonian originating cuneiform tablets concerning a dragon, is KUR, a word that can also be translated to literally mean *"mountain."* The name was lent to one of the oldest ziggurat temples, built in Nippur (NI.IBRU), and dedicated to the god Enlil: the E.KUR, or "House like a Mountain."

Throughout traditional global mythical lore, dragons literally inhabit the mountains—residing either deep within the very rocks or as a physical embodiment of the mountain itself. We see reflections of this belief in "magical incantations" used in modern practices to evoke dragon energy during rituals. For example, the "Evocation of the Dragon" ritual that appears in both the Pheryllt work by Douglas Monroe, in addition to the motion picture "Dragonslayer," is a Latin prose that speaks of the rocks of the mountain and the quintessential dragon spirit that resides within it.

THE LATIN "EVOCATION OF THE DRAGON"

Cum saxum saxorum,
In a duresum montum operaum da
in aet lutum inquinatum draconis

Nowhere and at no time has anyone in the modern New Age sought to understand this incantation—much like the *Charm of Making* translated in our foreword. Such *charms* are discarded by the skeptics as nonsense gibberish, but *we* know better.

Latin is an archaic language with few direct applications in the modern world—however, when required to take a foreign language in high school, I opted for Latin, hoping that it could assist my understanding of these types of charms. The notes I kept regarding the "Evocation of the Dragon" were not as conclusive as the *Charm of Making* eventually translated later with additional assistance. In fact, even with an elementary understanding of Latin, it was clear that incantations were often written phonetically—the way they sound—and it is possible that the 'predicates and tenses' require some configuring, and some of the later key words may still be wrong, I'm still going to share what I came up with.

"EVOCATION OF THE DRAGON" LATIN TRANS. NOTES

Cum saxum saxorum,
1. when the rock cliffs
2. with the rock cliffs

In a duresum montum operaum da
1. in a duress action of the mountain gives way
2. against the mountains works away

in aet lutum inquinatum draconis
1. set in soil the defiled dragon
2. set inside, the soiled earth-dragon

By the time of the "European Infestation"—our term for the Western migration of Dragon lore—artistic depictions of the energy evolved into new forms. No longer a catchall term applied to any infinite number of concepts and beings, the term "Dragon" (in western consciousness) developed into a specific icon: serpent-like, winged, two legs and two "arm" appendages. Consequently, new terminologies emerged to describe any number of semantic variations to this standard.

Suddenly, in Europe, the exotic zoological nature of Dragons developed varied definitions. The same creature, but without additional arm appendages, became known as a "Wyvern." A wyvern absent of any legs, a "Knucker." Better known, the wingless-knucker then became a "Worm," such as what is described at Loch Ness.

> DRAGON, serpent-like, wings, four-legged.
> WYVERN, serpent-like, wings, two-legged.
> KNUCKER, serpent-like, winged.
> WORM, serpent-like, usually sea-oriented.

Beyond even what we have described as the archetypal iconic dragon-figure, following a similar logic and motif of spawns of TIAMAT and other genetic manipulations from the Anunnaki, one is immediately led to wonder about the nature of other "fantastic" beasts and creatures described in the long-forgotten lore of ages past: the sphinx, the hydra, the minotaur, the gryphon and gargoyle—assuming what we "believe" concerning "dragons" to be true, what are we left to think concerning these other beings?

NexGen systemology studies propose that the program of life has a common and unifying origin. This hardly seems worth arguing—especially in the present context—but the idea that all life has been left to "naturally evolve" from what it was at its start to what it has become seems hard for even the "evolutionists" to swallow. There is a basic program or "seed of life" at the heart of all existence. When left uninhibited, progressive evolving life actually follows a very simple program of basic "cellular" reproduction—and this takes place for one specific purpose: *survival*. Environmental imprints and genetic information coding simply duplicate—shedding its skin to evolve into simply another "version" of itself, matching and duplicating—copy and pasting. Where is this in human history? With lightning quick speed after human inception we have seen no shortage in alterations and geographical adaptation when compared to even other "beasts of the field" that themselves, thanks to humans, can hardly be said to have lived and evolved unhindered existences.

Natural selection and basic evolutionary programs are valid, in their own respect, as a fundamental aspect of life-existence. But more than this, these programs are a necessity for the existence of all biological systems. But, humans, and most likely many of the other forms of life found in the cosmos, are not necessarily the result of purely "natural" evolution—as is the contemporary belief—but instead are manipulated via "alien intervention," meaning very simply "outside of itself," however one might choose to view or accept this semantic. Even a purist of our times using a Judeo-Christian perspective must agree that what is not naturally "terrestrial" to *this world*, must therefore be, by a relative standard: "alien" in nature. Alternate vocabulary throughout history includes terms like "angels" or "demons," not to mention the "dragons" of our current focus—but all have held religious connotations that, ethics and moral debates aside, all represent a very "alien" element to human consciousness. When we examine our natural surroundings, it leaves us to wonder—as William Blake did—is "religion" even a natural phenomenon? History would demonstrate that it too has been programmed, added to the systemology of the human condition from "outside sources."

By some interpretations of the migration of the *Dragon Tradition* from Sumeria to Europe, the focus becomes "blood"— often referred to as *dragonblood* or *dragon's blood*. Any preservation of these mysteries—such as the forms they survived as in Europe—appeared to be a threat to the structure of the new spiritual-political organization in power by that time: the Roman Empire—and eventually the Roman Catholic Church. In order for *them* to secure their own hold on "worldly power," all other claims to *The Dragon*—meaning the ancient seat of worldly power as "Divine Right" on earth—including those of specific lineages of "*dragonblood*," were thwarted or destroyed altogether. In brief: rather than risk the rise of potential enemies, all those who were suspect as opposition were killed.

Emphasis on the "Dragon Blood" living in the ancient lineages of Europe—including its priest-kings and dynasties—proved significant in preserving Sumerian, Babylonian, Egyptian and otherwise "Hermetic" mysteries of the ancients into "secret societies" and otherwise "underground occult schools" surviving to this day. "Demonization" of the Dragon by the Church forced those who chose to pursue these mysteries underground—and under the penalty of death! For thousands of years monopolized dictatorships governed freedom of true knowledge (and "gnosis"), preventing the masses from having direct experience with the Truth. What's more: there is sufficient existing "programming" within the human condition to prevent an accumulated and unified understanding of these things fully, as was intended by humanity's "creators."

Prior to the existence of ancient Babylonian and "Mardukite" traditions, little recorded knowledge of a Dragon Legacy may be found—other than loose associations with Enlilite-Anunnaki, meaning *Anu, Enlil* and *Enki*, and their involvement with early humans for their own purposes. "Fragmentation" of the loosely systematized pre-Babylonian (Sumerian) "unity" made the Dragon a representation of what is "forbidden" and/or "veiled" from the surface world—outside the domain of salient knowledge held by the surface realm and its inhabitants. The Dragon became a thing to be feared, or worse, the embodiment of all that was evil. Perhaps there is no finer application of the old adage that *people fear what they don't understand*—but in most respects, the *fear* manifests as *hate*. Such thoughts are beneath the studies of a true mystical Dragonmaster, which is undoubtedly the cover purpose that many venture into the pages of the *Draconomicon*.

ThE PhERYLLT PRIESThOOD
—ORIGINS Of ThE DRUIDS—

Various modern contemporary "New Age" movements have emerged, each reviving many niche interests from ages past— themes and *schemas* by which to approach "Reality." Each one draws from its own stream of esoteric and arcane mysteries. Each one attempts to tap the heart of a specific accessible—or even seemingly inaccessible—culture and *mythos*.

A conceptual or philosophical use of the *Dragon* is certainly no foreign matter throughout New Age esoteric revivals. Yet it cannot be said that the icon appears often to represent the field of actual "magick." It would seem to carry "fantastical" implications—representative of role-play and epic entertainment far more than serious occult pursuits. Perhaps in many respects, it has already been such a stretch for the mass consciousness of the present age to reintroduce the existence of magic—implying a re-enchantment of everyday life—that the incorporation of the *Dragon* is almost too far-reaching for even many modern day "magicians" and self-proclaimed "pagans."

But—of all factions of occult systemology revived today, there is one specifically that stands apart in matters of the *Dragon* and its legacy in Europe: the <u>Druids</u>.

In ancient Keltia—once dominating the majority of Europe— the Druid Order consisted of learned ones, those educated in Bardic Arts: cosmology and spirituality, natural-native history and geology, legendary history of heroes and mythology, healing and botanical medicine, astronomy and astrology, and of course "magic"—all of which were preserved, hidden in lines of Bardic verse and the researches of those who study them.

As primary loremasters of Celtic and Druid Mysteries, it is no wonder that Bardic Druids were considered the transmitter or catalyst of -awen- the essence, Divine Spark or spirit of inspiration that the Greeks termed "gnosis." It is to the ebb and flow of the -awen field- that the magical and poetic genius of the Druid is attributed.

Preservation of ancient knowledge is key among all elite orders of the ages. This Ancient Mystery School is timeless and spans all places on Earth. Past mystical cultures often relied on elite orders of scribe-priests, priestesses and poet-magicians to bridge ancestral roots and traditions with the future— esoteric organizations rooted in 'languages', 'communication', and above all the written word. The poetic genius of "awen"— the *Divine Spark of Cosmic Creation*—manifests throughout all creative arts and even as the spirit of "prophecy," an ability to observe experiences with a heightened awareness and communicate it in the World of Form. Druidism is, therefore, an echo of this "poetic genius," an amalgamation of collected knowledge preserved by the ancient elite, including a mystical and scientific understanding of the world that eluded the perceptual range of "common folk."

For thousands of years, since the height of their power in *Keltia*, the entire subject of the *Druids* has been enshrouded in mystique and misinformation—much like the *Dragon* itself. Among these aspects of interest to Celtic, or more specifically "Druidic" revival, is the *Pheryllt Priesthood*, an ancient Welsh "organization" known in legend as the "*Dragon Alchemists*." As our legends continue: the *Pheryllt* were based in the mountaintops of ancient Snowdonia in Wales—a place where "communion" with the "Sky Gods" is most accessible, particularly if by way of their representative ambassadors: the *Dragons!*

> "Oxford is old, even in England... its foundations date from Alfred, and even from King Arthur, if, as is alleged, the Pheryllt of the Druids had a seminary there."
> —Ralph Waldo Emerson.

The Pheryllt represent an element of "Celtic" history that is not altogether the same as the "contemporary neopagan Celtic Druidism" that many seekers might be better acquainted with as the result of popular materials. While there are some aspects that do appear one-to-one with the often-biased perspectives offered in the Roman literary renderings, the vision of the Pheryllt is reminiscent more of the archetypal wizard and priestly-magician image than that carried by later Druids, which appear to have become a governmental organization to guide and unify the Celtic nations as a whole. Such was not the original intention or functional purpose of the Pheryllt alone. If we consider the distantly remote chronology of pre-Druidic Pheryllt residence in prehistoric Britain, this is concurrent with what could even be an extension of the same "scientific" and "mystical" work conducted in pre-dynastic Mesopotamia, specifically by *Enki* in his proto-Sumerian home of *Eridu*, or even later by *Marduk* in *Babylon*, all of which were at one time or another represented by the *Dragon*.

Origins of Druidry, the "Danubian tribes," and specifically the group of Pheryllt that isolated themselves in the Welsh mountains, has all remained quite mysterious in traditional history. Leading theories have included everything from the north to the south and all in between. Words like "Hyperborean" are thrown around—others have professed a literal interpretation of Plato's *Atlantis*. Many have cited the "Iberian Peninsula" or modern-day Spain as a genetic source of the "Beaker People," a neolithic culture that is allegedly present when Stonehenge is constructed. Even these people would have migrated there, westward from the Mediterranean or Danube River Valley, and Iberian scripts tend to resemble a primitive hybrid combination of Celtic *Ogham* and Norse *Runes*.

There is sufficient reason to plant Mesopotamia as the distant source of the Pheryllt Dragon Tradition. By the time of recorded Druidic histories, the Greek and post-dynastic Egyptian Hermetic traditions had already begun to affect how the Great Mysteries were interpreted. The simplicity of a *primum mobus* move in consciousness to fragment and relay the "totality" of the tradition in Babylon was only further and further fractured by socio-political or otherwise religious interpretations of emerging and human populations in civilizations of differing languages and cultural backgrounds all over the world. It was usually only to the most remote and secluded locales that the Mystery Tradition was brought and we can glean our most undefiled examples. Even as the oldest recorded versions of the Atlantean Flood-Myth have actually emerged from Mesopotamia—those that were imported by the Egyptians and the Greeks, especially Plato—we can ascribe the same origins then to the Pheryllt, a knowledge tradition and Dragon legacy that continues to perpetuate the same esoteric cycles of mystery.

Most publicly significant literary records of the Druids would unfortunately require us to lend the Romans an ear. A problem arises here in their being the archenemy of the Druids, putting forth a millennium of political propaganda to thwart out the existence of the Druid Tradition, not to mention the rape and murder of later Druidesses and their priests during the era of Roman invasion. But the *Dragon* could not be truly annihilated—its image still seen in blood red, gracing the national Welsh flag. In ancient Wales, the Pheryllt Druids were known as "Dragons" themselves—a title once adopted by all Druids and equated in the animal kingdom to serpents and snakes. In the time of St. Patrick, once the Druid legacy had been excluded to Ireland by efforts of the Milesians and later Romans, he considered the final annihilation of Druids and the public presence of the Dragon Legacy as an act of ridding the isle of "snakes"—and therein the archetypal dragonslaying image is once again used to shift public consciousness.

The Pheryllt are presented in Bardic literature as the "first systematizers of the ancient Cymry" (*Cymry* meaning the Welsh Celts) and their knowledge or wisdom-based tradition. Given such a description the seeker is reminded of the "first systematizers" of global knowledge as an archetype, which can be found in Mesopotamia.

The modern "Mardukite" *New Thought* movement may be seen publicly with its obvious slant toward Mesopotamian emphasis, yet at the same time, those members of the Mardukite Research Organization that contributed to its early development were also those simultaneously interested in its connection to the Pheryllt/Druidic paradigm—and thus its members may be often found to have interests or be involved with revival practices of both, and without contradiction. As a "New Thought" methodology of "systemology" that is grounded in both logic and wide-sweeping antiquated esoteric literature, the parameters are equally wide and require wide vision to behold. It is no secret that this "movement" has come up against much debate and controversy, even among self-proclaimed "open-minded enlightenment seekers" of the "truth." And yet when forced to examine the lore and histories *Self-Honestly*, removing the goggles or colored-glasses that filter perception and reception of reality experience, the task seems too difficult for even many of these "New Age" types.

Perhaps one of the first subjects of "controversy" connecting the *Druids*, *Pheryllt* and *Dragons* is: Stonehenge. Located on a hillside of Salisbury Plain (England), this 'circle' or 'henge' of stones remains one of the most infamous "ancient mysteries." Debate over whether or not *Druids* literally "built" Stonehenge concerned historians for a long time. Regardless of the time-line issues between construction of Stonehenge and existence of the organized *Celtic Druids* (that we are most familiar with by classical writings), it seems matter-of-fact that local *Druids* at the very least *used* Stonehenge—regardless of its original design and purpose. Of course, the local legends of England often have attributed construction of Stonehenge to "Merlyn" (else *Myrddin* or *Merlin*), specifically the one from the Arthurian period—as this title was carried by several persons—but this too would support a significant time-line issue. King Arthur's era is c. 5th Century AD and construction of Stonehenge is thousands of years prior to this. The structure clearly marks the sun's rise during a turn or shift of the observed celestial (zodiac) time to the Age of Aries—in c. 2160 B.C.

Pheryllt Druidism, as it is originally recorded, is likened to *alchemy*, a science named for the land of "khem," the "black lands" of Egypt. It is later classified literally as the "black arts" of science, imported from Mesopotamia to the Mediterranean by way of Egyptian Hermetic tradition. These arts are more often expressed philosophically in Druidism—and many other popular facets of "New Age" ritualism and magic—in the form of "Elementalism," which is say: pertaining to the "elements" of Nature, or else the "natural forces" of the universe. At some juncture or another, these "energy currents" themselves, as well as the natural forms and cosmic background reality of the universe that the magician is working to *manipulate*, are all referred to, at one time or another, as the *Dragon*.

The idea that the Great Mystery can be "coiled" and "veiled" in countless layers of mystery—and "levels" of understanding —is, by definition, the very nature of the *Dragon* and the *dragonmind*. This means that it is the very existence of The Dragon as the first-form, and the programming of the cosmos with the dragonmind, that in essences makes the "occult" and related esoteric pursuits possible. Not only such, it makes the manifold geometric and mathematical forms possible in our Realm of Light, where ordered patterns of "chaotic" *shapes* and *forms* occupy the whole of our reality experience.

Lewis Spence, the esoteric historian, explored the Welsh Mysteries of the Pheryllt in his classic treatise, 'Secret Traditions of Ancient Britain', where he writes:—

> In the "Book of Taliesin" we encounter a group still more important from the mystical point of view, that of Keridwen, her hideous son Avagddu, his sister Creirwy, and his brother Morvran. So that Avagddu, the ugly, may be compensated by the possession of supernatural knowledge, Keridwen prepares a cauldron of inspiration which must be brewed for a year, and which produce three drops of divine fluid. She sets a servant, Gwion, to watch it, and the three drops falling on his finger, he

conveys it to his mouth and becomes inspired. Keridwen, in her anger, pursues him, and as he assumes various forms, a hare, a fish, and a grain of wheat, in his flight, she takes on the shape of a greyhound, an otter, and at last a hen, in which she swallows the grain, later bearing Gwion as a child, whom she abandons to the sea in a coracle. The child she abandons to the waves becomes, later, Taliesin, the magical bard.

The Druidic bards who lived and sang under the Welsh princes unanimously represent Keridwen as presiding over the hidden mysteries of their ancient cult. Cynddelw, who flourished in the twelfth century, sings: "How mysterious were the ways of the songs of Keridwen! How necessary to understand them in their true sense!" Llywarch ap Llywelyn, wrote between 1160 and 1220, asks for "inspiration as if it were from the Cauldron of Keridwen," and says that he will address his lord "with the dowry of Keridwen, the Ruler of Bardism." It was essential for those bards who aspired to the Chair of Song to have tasted the waters of inspiration from her cauldron, to have been initiated into her mysteries. That the myth of Keridwen is all-important in our quest may be gathered from a passage from the Book of Taliesin:

> "Then Keridwen determined, agreeably to the mystery of the Books of Pheryllt, to prepare for her son a cauldron of water of inspiration and knowledge... In the meantime, Keridwen, with due attention to the Books of Astronomy, and to the hours of the planets, employed herself daily in collecting plants of every species, which preserved any rare virtues... She stationed Gwion the Little, the son of Gwreany the Herald of Llanvair, in Powys, the land of rest, to superintend the preparation of the cauldron."

The Pheryllt, according to whose ritual she proceeded, are frequently mentioned by the bards of Wales, and an old chronicle, quoted by Dr. Thomas Williams, states that the Pheryllt had a college at Oxford prior to the foundation of that University. These Pheryllt appear to have been a section of the Druidic brotherhood, teachers and scientists, skilled in all that required the agency of fire, hence the name has frequently been translated "alchemists" or "metallurgists." Indeed, chemistry and metallurgy are known as "*Celvyddydan Pheryllt*," or "the arts of the Pheryllt," who would seem to have had as their headquarters the city of Emrys in the district of Snowdon, famous for its magical associations, the city of the dragons of Beli.

Somewhere in the district of Snowdon lie the remains of this ancient British city of Emrys, or "the ambrosial city," also known in Welsh tradition as the city of Dinas Affaraon, or "the higher powers." To this mysterious community the poems of the Welsh bards allude so frequently as to place its actual existence beyond all question. Not only is it mentioned in the "Black Book of Caermarthen" and other Cymric manuscripts as the centre of mystical rites, but it is alluded to by one of Camden's commentators as occupying the summit of "the panting cliff" on Snowdon itself. Davies says that it stood "upon the road from the promontory of Lleyn to that part of the coast which is opposite Mona" (Anglesey), and Gibson, in his work on Camden, identifies it with the ruins of an exceedingly strong fortification encompassed by a triple wall on an eminence called Broich y Ddinas, "the ridge of the city," which forms part of the summit of Penmaen, seated on the top of one of the highest mountains of that part of Snowdon which lie toward the sea.

In Emrys were concealed in the time of Bile the solar deity, and in the time of Prydain the son of Aedd the

Great, the dragons which are so frequently referred to as harnessed to the car of Keridwen, so it appears not improbable that the city was in some manner associated with her mysteries. Davies believed that the Pheryllt were priests of those mysteries in the ambrosial city of Emrys. Now what, precisely, is the significance of the goddess Keridwen and her mystical cauldron? Mythically speaking, the vessel in question was designed for the preparation of a brew which induced inspiration and awoke the prophetic and bardic faculties. The myth is an allegory of initiation, of which the tasting of the water was an essential rite.

In the "Book of Taliesin" a number of ingredients are enumerated which went to compose the mystical elixir brewed in the Cauldron of Keridwen, the Pair Pumwydd, the "Cauldron of the Five Trees," so-called in allusion to the five particular trees or plants requisite to the preparation. Certain Cymric legends represent this Pair as a bath, the water of which conferred immortality, but deprived the bather of utterance – an allusion, perhaps, to the oath of secrecy administered prior to initiation. Elsewhere, Taliesin alludes to it as "the Cauldron of the Lord of the Deep," and states that it will not boil the food of him who is not bound by his oath.

The Welsh Bards made use in their initiatory rites of a decoction of plants or herbs which they believed could bestow certain powers of inspiration, eloquence, prophecy, and song upon those who partook of it. The ingredients of Keridwen's cauldron, which, according to Taliesin, contained berries, the foam of the ocean, cresses, wort and vervain which had grown high and kept apart from the influence of the moon. The residue of the water in the cauldron of Keridwen was, as we have seen, poisonous and accursed, that is, it was symbolically supposed to contain the sins and pollutions of the novitiates, and was cast out...

When we reflect on the more readily conceivable aspects of the Dragon energy present in the Pheryllt legends and resulting natural, botanical and zoological interpretations, then modern generalized terms like "wyvern" or "knucker" pale in comparison to the more spiritual or metaphysical—otherwise "elemental"—attributes that "Dragons" may actually possess. Whether referring to the literal genetic manipulation of hybrid biological entities or an allegorical mixing of chemical components to affect natural courses of energy on the planet, the emphasis of the Pheryllt—and the later Druids (and Celts) —became wholly focused on Nature's "elements." Elementally speaking, we can correspond cardinal (primary) dragon-forms as given in Druidic lore comparably as follows:

DRAIG-TALAMH – Earth Element (*Knuckers*)
DRAIG-ATHAR – Air Element (*Dragons and Drakes*)
DRAIG-TEINE – Fire Element (*Wyverns and Drakes*)
DRAIG-UISGE – Water Element (*Worms*)

Where practical ritual (ceremonial) and religious (spiritual) subjects and applications enter the equation—especially with regard to classification of natural elements—we have at once put our foot in another forum of debate. In this case, one that concerns quantitative fragmentation of the All-as-One universal (cosmic) order—which can actually be "realized" as holistic paradigms with any number of divisions—dualism, trinities, and so forth. Some purists believe the Celts (and as such, the Druids) adhered to a strict threefold cosmic division of only three elements, thereby dismissing references to any system that does not further this point. And how close-minded is this: when the Druids themselves made efforts to migrate far and wide to all reaches of the known world during their quest to unify the whole of universal knowledge. We should, today, place no limitations on what our ancestors were truly capable of—and no restriction on our pursuits to recover the lost keys to their treasure trove of cosmic wisdom and true power.

MERLYN AND ThE DRAGONS
—A LEGACY OF DRUIDS—

MERLYN... DRAGONS... Archetypes of the ancient world—those which have long rung true and deep in our consciousness—will ever remain with us, even to this day, so long as there are *Guardians* of this wisdom still living. The works of contemporary fantasy art also offer us no leeway here: dragons and wizards *go together.*

We are moving through time now, departing from lessons of the most distant past, Dragons of Sumeria and the global rise of ancient tradition in remote places. The iconic image we carry of "Merlyn and the Dragons" comes to us from a more recently point in our history—but a critical time for the preservation of the Dragon Tradition: the rise and domination of the Church, just prior to—and actually causing the inception of—civilization plummeting into the *Dark Ages.*

As a classic archetypal wizard or archmage, Merlyn appears in Celtic and Druidic mythos, later incorporated into the Arthurian cycle permanently—made popular in the New Age as an instructional model. Of course, not everyone believes Merlyn (also "Merlin") was a historical figure. Many uninitiated hold a belief that he is a fictional-fantasy figure created for Arthurian romance tales. Others, slightly more open-minded, believe that the great wizard did exist in some past age, but that the time for "magic" has since passed us by and the Merlyn-current is at best, a distant, long forgotten and inaccessible facet of genetic memory. While it seems only natural for a modern student to take similar strides in differentiating between the historical and fantasy depictions of Merlyn, the symbolic and spiritual validity of both forms remains equally powerful.

The challenge in identifying the character stereotypically associated with Merlyn is that there are countless discrepancies among accounts. Geoffrey of Monmouth offers the first significant literary descriptions of the mage in a section of *"History of the British Kings"* (1136) called the *"Prophecies of Merlyn."* Triad verses, similar to quatrains of Nostradamus, detail various phases of warfare and changes in kingship that affect Britain from the age of Arthur until the "Apocalypse." Although synchronization of history to these prophecies has mainly gone unrecognized, neodruid R.J. Stewart illuminated diverse symbolism (animal, numerological, etc.) in his *"Prophetic Vision of Merlin"* (1986). After completing his accounts on the kings, Geoffrey returns to the subject of Merlyn, seeking to relay a more complete sketch of the wizard's identity. This companion work is known as the *"Vita Merlini"* or the *"Life of Merlyn,"* which R.J. Stewart also annotated as the release of *"Mystic Life of Merlin"* (1986). The two texts became a cornerstone for modern Arthurian-neodruidic following. Original versions of both complete texts appear in Joshua Free's recension of the *Book of Pheryllt;* an abridged version appears in *Appendix B.*

The name "Merlyn" comes from the Welsh name "Myrddin." There is little difficulty finding references to these names historically. There are many. So many, in fact, that it is difficult sometimes to distinguish one persona from another. Classical accounts specifically refer to both a Myrddin Emrys (Merlinus Ambrosus), the famous 5-6th Century Druid mentor of Arthur; and also Myrddin Wyllt (Merlinus Caledonius), the 6-7th Century mage who made most of his public appearances in Scotland. There are so many other vague references that some folks question whether or not "Merlyn" is a proper name, or simply a title. Could it be possible that the "Merlyn" was a role or function in Druidic society—like an "ArchDruid"—later misinterpreted throughout the shadows of history?

The "Merlyn" role may have exclusive connections to Dragon Kings, else as their advisors. Merlyns are all Hermetic practitioners, and like Hermes, connected to the serpent of wisdom.

This later is identified with the owl of knowledge, Merlyn's familiar: Archimedes. According to "*Vita Merlini*," Merlyn did possess a familiar, but it was not an owl. During his residence in the forest, a place that the "mad man" frequently sought to center, ground and regain his sanity away from civilization, Merlyn became close friends with a wolf. At another point of emotional distress he is depicted riding a stag. As the "wild wizard of the woods," Merlyn is generally distinguished as a "Master of Animals." Not only does this qualify his shamanic Druid nature, it displays an inclination for the human spark of consciousness to return to the wilderness. When loved ones died in futile battles and the counseled refused to hear his words unto their own doom, Merlyn would get frustrated with the world of men for a time and retire to the woodlands.

In every example of the "Merlyn" persona, he exists at some point as adviser to a king. This may actually clue us in to the cardinal function of the "Merlyn." Rumored as having a non-human father, Myrddin Emrys was sought out as a young boy by a drunken materialistic Welsh king named Vortigern who had been having difficulties erecting his castle on a particular hillside, called "Dinas Ffaraon" (or "Pharaon" named for the Pheryllt). The walls kept collapsing, even in spite of the ridiculous advice to use the blood from sacrifices in the mortar. Merlyn received a vision of two dragons beneath the hill, a red and a white, engaged in mortal combat, each devouring the other by the tail. The eventual death of the red dragon in the vision was a symbol to Merlyn that Vortigern himself would lose control to King Uther, Arthur's future father. This came to pass as expected and the vision solidified Merlyn's connection to both dragons and seership, prophecy and divination.

Merlyn's prophetic vision for the future reveals dragons heralding a time of change. A perceptive student will discover key parallels between this mass-transformation and older Anunnaki-Nephilim lore concerning the fate of mankind. Merlyn's vision of a Gate to the Outside parallels Mesopotamian lore. Disruption of natural order and shifts in stellar (star) patterns (and the zodiac) are indicative of an axis shift and/or change in fields on the Earth Planet, also predicted by the Mayan and Hopi "End of Days" or end of the "long count of days." A subverted polarity shift of "above" and "below" (Hermetic) is mirrored in the prediction that "root" and "branch" will trade places, denoting a collision of the physical and the invisible dimensions. This could force or focus the human consciousness to vibrate at a new level of manifesting capabilities, and would require one to possess preexisting esoteric skills, emotional temperance and wisdom to effectively master. The following are some examples of these prophetic triads:—

"THE PROPHECIES OF MERLYN" — SELECTED TRIADS

(58) In the Shadow of London
Shall a Serpent emerge which shall
Be the Annihilation of Mankind.

(67) A Worm, with Fire for Breath
Shall Incinerate the Trees. From the Vapor and Smoke
Comes Seven Lions with Heads of a Goat.

(82) A Knight in Armor comes forth
Flying on the Back of a Dragon. He holds the
Body and Tail of the Dragon in his hands.

(87a) The Stars are confounded,
Turning their Eyes from the Earth,
Destined to follow New Courses.

(87b) Crops will wither and die as
No precipitation comes from the
Heavens to nourish them.

(88a) Root and Branches shall instantly Change Places
As the Light of the Sun is occulted by Mercury
And the Helm of Mars calls to Venus.

(89a) Mars causes a Shadow to fall and the
Range of Mercury moves beyond its Natural Orbit.
Orion unsheathes his Sword.

(89b) Phoebus perturbs the Clouds.
Jupiter and Venus move beyond
The Range of their Natural Orbits.

(90) The Sickle of Saturn sweeps
Away Mankind and the Houses of the
Zodiac weeps for the Visions of this Rage.

The legacy of Merlyn remains alive in the present era. All accounts concerning his life leave the subject of his death wide open. In most versions, he is trapped in a "crystalline dimension," frozen in time, maintaining an inanimate but conscious existence. Some stories allude to a "secret observatory" in the woods where he retired. Others speak of a witch-deity (Morgan) using Merlyn's lover Vivian as a tool to trap him. Another similar figure, Morgan le Fey or "Morgana of the Faerie," is described as a half-brother to Arthur who tricks Merlyn into using his own magic against him. Not one account reveals a "happily-ever-after" ending for this great mage.

No contemporary wizards believe that Merlyn is completely gone. The state he resides in still allows for his energy and spiritual (astral) presence to be called forth in magick. Similar energetic currents and stories exist concerning shades of Ascended Masters, Hermes, Baphomet and even Christian Rosenkreutz (the famous Rosicrucian)—all of which are still very much "alive" in the New Age: "Not dead, but dreaming."

The archetypal Merlyn-current still exists for those practitioners who feel an individual calling towards this path. While it seems logical to view the historical Merlyn as a Druid, the Merlyn-current is not only restricted to neodruidism. Pherylltphobic practitioners often believe that most modern Merlyn-obsessed individuals are simply misguided students of Douglas Monroe's brand of neo-Pheryllt revival. But recent incorporation of the Merlyn-current appears throughout the Hermetic revival. Before breaking off to form a separate faction, the "Merlin Temple" once existed within the Hermetic Order of the Golden Dawn (GD) system in the 1940s. These practitioners were serious students of the Golden Dawn, like Dion Fortune, that felt a personal connection with Druidic and Arthurian (European) archetypal images as opposed to the more classical Egyptian and Greek flavors prominent in the GD. Later, the lore was integrated into another GD faction called the Stella Matutina (SM) or "Order of the Morning Star."

Connecting with the Merlyn-current is an easy feat for the experienced New Age mystic. In addition to calling his name in rituals, or using the bluish-silver "Merlyn Current"—or ray of light—Arthurian archetypes are usually channeled via meditation and visualization. Attributes, personality and energetic quality of any mythic figure can be ritually assimilated. Care should be taken whenever channeling or invoking, even with beneficent intelligences. Other more "psychological" techniques also exist.

The "Empty Chair" method requires sitting across from an (literally) empty chair that one will use as the focus. The operator enters the body of light, balances their chakras and strengthens the auric field. A mental impulse is then directed to communicate with the energy or ray, like a phone call. Once the "call" is received and the energy channeled, it is focused at the empty chair where a figure (Merlyn) is visualized. A similar technique is used whenever calling elementals to the nemeton, "mandala" or sacred ritual/ceremonial "circle."

Modern Druid lore and its revival tradition is often based on the Merlyn archetype. A seeker even reads legends of Druids may that have been able to mystically hibernate, extending their lifespan that allowed for widely dispersed appearances in society at critical junctures. This is sometimes called the "Druid's Sleep." Furthermore, lore suggests an Astral Body of a "Druid Master" can remain accessible to mentor future apprentices. Legends refer to this as a "Druid Shade." Certainly both of these facets relate directly to the mystical tradition of the Merlyn-current.

Since the most ancient times—when technology and magic of gods coexisted with the "Realm of Men"—there has been no other Western World figure more strongly resonating with true Hermetic mysteries than the archetypal Druidic wizard-magician Merlyn. Accounts of his mystic life—whether historical or legendary—reflect personal initiation to all paths found on the "Tree of Life" and a direct connection to all traditional archetypes of the Tarot.

Modern neo-Pheryllt practitioners have proposed connecting with the "Shade" of Merlyn using the epitaph found on a 6th Century gravestone standing near Mount Newais or Newhill. The suggestion of the verse does not, of course, come without skepticism by anti-Pheryllt neo-druids. It does, however, appear in the Welsh Peniarth MS. 98B: *Englynion y Beddau*, "The Stanzas of the Graves." A specific suggested incense formula: 1 part wormwood, 2 parts datura and 3 parts yew bark, follows the old adage: "an herb, a flower and a tree." Given the Necromantic nature of the rite—connecting with ancestral spirits—a circle of "carved heads" is set to mark the nemeton or ritual space. Gourds and turnips are suggested in *"The 21 Lessons of Merlyn"* (1992), although skeptics somehow misinterpreted its author's comment: "today, we carve pumpkins" as "ancient Druids carved pumpkins," which even Monroe admits is false.

The epitaph is provided here for personal experimentation. You might also try incorporating suggestions for similar practices from other traditions and systems of "magick." Although these types of evocation seem typical of Samhain, esoteric lore also indicates that the Beltane Gate is actually more accessible from "our" side, at the exactly opposite "peak" of the year.

Another suggestion is to access the Astral Plane for all forms of spiritual evocation. This is both safer and more effective than waiting out in the cold for "physical apparitions" while suffocating on smoke plumes. In the case of the "Empty Chair" technique, an apparition is wholly visualized as a means of connecting more directly with "unseen" energies. This does not mean that it is impossible for an energy to concentrate enough to reveal physical effects, but this tends to be wasteful of the potential active use of energy, as is evident in other known operations of "conjuration to physical appearance."

"EVOCATION OF MERLYN'S SHADE" — WELSH EPITAPH

Bed an ap llian ymnewais
(*beth ahn ahp t'lie-in eem-new-eyes*)
The grave of the nun's son on Newais:

Vynyd [fynydd] lluagor Llew Emreis
(*feen-ith, th'loo-ah-or th-loo eem-rays*)
Mountain of Battle ["warlord"], Llew [lion of] Emrys,

Prif ddrewin, Myrddin Emreis
(*preeve, dew-in, Meer-thin Ehm-rays*)
Chief Magican, Merlyn Emrys

ThE RISE Of ThE DRAGONS
—A LEGACY Of DRAGONS—

After systematization of human civilization—efforts launched in ancient Babylonia—the Dragon became esoterically connected to all things powerful and divine. Whether it was stars or star-gods—or the messengers and stewards of their ways—the people came to respect the Dragon as a symbol of sovereignty and kingship. This was accomplished first in Babylon with the *Sirrush* dragon as royal pet of its Mardukite pantheon coupled with heavenly dragonslaying alluded to in the *Enuma Elis*—all of which sealed the iconic impression in people's minds. When battle for worldly control fell to the Church, it was the *dragon* that was "demonized" as a representation of all that had stood in the way of their own rise to power—everything "pagan."

Previous sections from the current "grimoire of the dragon"—presented to the world as the *Draconomicon*—already have introduced varied ideas regarding the nature of the Dragon: as an allusion to the "universe" holistically; the physical "earth" planet; potentially another distant "planet"; powerful beings which came from the "stars" as "alien" forces or "Sky Gods"; and, even the distantly prehistoric "dinosaurs" and "mythic" beasts that we actually know very little about directly. By the time of the Dark Ages, however, the Dragon primarily represented one fundamental thing above all else: divinely ordained kingship and worldly control—hence, the rise of Dragon Kings.

The title "Dragon King" was not arbitrary or without deep underlying meanings. Dragon Kings were named such because they were either initiated into secret schools of forbidden knowledge and/or carried a physical "bloodline" lineage of genetic memory—both of which were links to an unbroken line of the Dragon Legacy since it had first been realized on Earth, thousands of years ago. Semantic connections to the Druids, Anunnaki, or even distant Asian continental emperors, may all be drawn. Though otherwise completely "human" in appearance, the genetics—and therefore, "genetic memory"—was thought to be different, or to contain different "information" than the "average" ("normal") population masses.

The Dragon Kings were set apart from the mass population that they *led*—and the masses recognized a quality in these individuals that entitled them to lead. We are speaking in general terms, of course, as not all of them were equally qualified or best chosen to lead. The time of the ancient "alien," draconic or reptilian "gods" had come and gone, leaving in their stead a very specific "dynastic" and "royal" succession to be followed, alongside which, we see a unique class of Dragonmaster magicians, wizards, mystics and priestesses that all reinforce the political position and spiritual infrastructure of the "Realm." The "Dark Ages" represent a time when this was no longer the case—when the ancient pact between men and gods was no longer observed, and the militant and political power of the Roman Church entered the picture.*

When the earth was plunged into the ignorant reality imposed by the Church, the *Dragons* were instantly demonized into devils and demons—and along with it, the entire legacy of Druids and Mardukite Babylonians as *Dragons*. The act of dragonslaying remained a "godly" one—ordained by the heavens—now a decree of the Judeo-Christian God as entrusted to the Church, and mirrored in the actions of some of the more prestigious saints and deities of Medieval Europe including Saint George and Archangel Saint Michael. Any references to the Dragon in Judeo-Christian scriptures (Leviathan, Behemoth, &tc.) were all now officially connected to "evil" and heretical pre-Christian or "pagan" blasphemous ideals—all of which were to be avoided as pit-traps of the "Devil," or better still, destroyed!

---

* See also the original *Mardukite Liber-D* discourse, released popularly as *"Book of Elven-Faerie"* by Joshua Free.

On a more metaphorical and spiritual "level" of understanding, the conflict between humans and dragons—or even with the two dragons, archetypal of the story of Merlyn's current and Pheryllt Alchemy—represents a microcosm and macrocosm of activity throughout the interconnected "Universe."

The disharmony and unrest reflective in our relationship with the dragon—and dragons with other dragons—is that which exists within us and all around us. We are each a reflection of our own universe, and as such, we project or emanate this energy outwardly and continuously conform reality existence to our own universe. Only when the individual is at rest—in the awareness of *Self*—at peace, that the whole of the world's perceived spiritual imbalances and political struggles can find rest. This is all-encompassing lesson, critical to the very existence, survival and evolution of humans on the planet, far beyond the mere "taming" of the "inner dragon."

One key concept, idea or theme surrounding the Dragon—is "*guardianship*." Many symbols connected to the Dragon Legacy are considered "guardian objects" or power symbols found in relevant demonstrations of political-magic (of the "state") and spiritual-magic (of the "wizarding" class). Once again—looking back through remote esoteric annals of time, even before the classical era and works of the far east, it is Mesopotamia and records of the ANUNNAKI that we can attribute to its origins. Spreading from the ancient near east and Mediterranean, the symbolic Dragon archetypes of "worldly power" became universal icons: "on earth as it is in heaven."

It is not surprising that with the corruption of systems and human civilization as a whole, we now attribute most "traditional" aspect of the Dragon Kings as signs of wealth. Yet, our "royalties" observed today are little more than 'status icons', figureheads earning lip-service—far from a self-honest preservation of dynastic bloodlines (genetic memory). Prior to their adoption by a more "worldly" organization of Dragon Kings—items of Power: the crown; the wand; the staff or scepter; the holy sword; precious necklaces; body ornaments; and specific jewels or gemstones—all shared a historic occult legacy related to the *Dragon*, and it is even possible that in more distant times, an altogether different (and more pragmatic or technological) purpose for such devices may have existed. By the time of the Medieval era, any true sense of function or genuine sacredness fell by the wayside, overtaken by much more mundane, material and political values—those still present in the human psyche today. With true meanings of all symbolism lost, we find a specific demographic of the population—often apart or outside the population—dedicated to esoteric mysteries, recovering the lost scientific knowledge and spiritual technologies known thousands of years ago, those still left to be rediscovered today, or relinquished from the hands of those in power that are ultimately unworthy to be "stewards" of this planet.

During the "Dark Ages," use of *Dragon* symbols to represent worldly power were made famous through wide usage, but it certainly did not originate there. Referring back to our most ancient written records—clay cuneiform tablets from sands of Mesopotamia—there are references of battle and warfare for control of the "ME" (or MEs), pronounced "*may*"—elsewhere in the lore referred to as "divine decrees," among which included critical data known as the "Arts of Civilization." These facets of knowledge seem critical for maintaining organized (global) authority—a design covertly laden in our records of the past, particularly concerning *Anunnaki*—the archaic and forgotten origins of the Dragon Legacy.

Control of the "ME" and/or "Divine Decrees" runs parallel to symbols of the *Dragon* representing the global authority of the "younger generation" of *Anunnaki* "gods"—especially *Marduk* in *Babylon* and also the goddess *Inanna-Ishtar* who maintained a wide-sweeping influence within *Mesopotamia* and beyond, making her way directly—under various languages/names—in the Egyptian, Greek, Semitic and other systems derived from the Dragon Legacy of the *Ancient Near East*.

As explained in *Mardukite Liber-50:*[*]

"Assyrian art often depicts *Inanna-Ishtar* with wings. The same winged form is visible on her Egyptian form as *Isis*. Clearly she was a goddess of the aerial world, not only the *"Anunit-(um)"* (or *"Anu's Beloved"*), but literally a "queen" of the skies, stars and/or heavens. Mythological cycles describe seven objects connected to *Ishtar* for her astral travels. Similarly, there are seven garments and ornaments removed during her *"Descent to the Underworld."* It is quite likely that these items are related to her position as "Lady of the Stars" or "Queen of Heaven"—power symbols associated with this role. Mystical revivalists consider this symbolism significant for modern ritual magic activities reviving Mesopotamian-based ceremonialism (and the Underworld), but perhaps they have a greater unseen esoteric relevance."

In Ishtar's "Crossings to the Underworld"—given in *"The Complete Anunnaki Bible"*[‡] —these objects are referred to as seven "Divine Decrees" that she "fixes" to her body very specifically.

THE STAR-DRAGON REGALIA OF INANNA-ISHTAR

1. Shugurra, Starry Crown of Anu—on her head
2. Wand of Lapis Lazuli—in her hand
3. Necklace of Lapis Lazuli—around her neck
4. Bag of Brilliant-Shinning-Stones—on her belt
5. Gold Ring of Power—on her finger
6. Frontlet Amulet—as a breastplate
7. Pala, Garments of the Queen of Heaven—worn

---

[*] Available in paperback as *"The Sumerian Legacy: A Guide to Esoteric Archaeology"* or in the hardcover anthology *"Gates of the Necronomicon: The Secret Anunnaki Tradition of Babylon"* by Joshua Free.

[‡] Also available in hardcover as *"Necronomicon: The Anunnaki Bible"* edited by Joshua Free, or as the abridged paperback pocket edition.

In reflection of descriptions found on our most ancient literary cycles, kingship—and worldly authority and domination—represented a "mastery of the dragon." This was even sometimes, though not always, demonstrated physically during the *Dark Ages* with elaborate "mock" dragonslaying ceremonies—public rituals that kings were expected to participate in, so as to prove their sovereignty (guardianship and dominance) over the "Realm"--a name given to all that was literally "real" within the domain of the King.

If we consider the original Druidic use of the "burning figure" that we are mostly aware of only by Roman accounts as the "Wicker Man," it is actually a *Dragon*, burned during public Celtic "fire-festival" observances—and again, to demonstrate a symbol of authoritative power of Dragon Kings and the cosmic wisdom of Dragon Priests and Druidesses. It should be understood that in the ancient Druid (or Pheryllt) tradition, this Dragon is not burned in effigy as an "evil" spirit, but rather, in glory of the Dragon and what it represented on every "level."

As the time of gods led into a time of men, the ancient and forgotten sciences—and even elaborate means of warcraft—were laid to waste in place of the almighty sword. What could be more powerful to represent the governance of men over men —or part-human-part-divine kings over men—then the sword, a fiery weapon that could not only end a man's own life, but also represented the fundamental forces of all life: the Dragon. For what is the worth of a dragonslaying icon without the "means" to actually do it, a means which—according to some dragon lore—could originally have been a spear in ancient times, before evolving to the sword. Yet, in either case, we are confronted with an icon that also represents the submergence of mass consciousness into an industrious iron-age—cold, dark and unyielding.

The Arthurian literary cycles describe several mystic swords, although they are now typically lumped together as one. For example, the "Sword-in-the-Stone" is not actually the same as legendary "Excalibur" in many of the accounts. Where the one was "magically" placed in a boulder (or anvil in some versions) to await its rightful carrier, the other one is actually bestowed upon the boy-king from the "Lady of the Lake"—a figure from the Celtic Mythos. In the 1981 motion picture "Excalibur," this confusion is dramatically resolved with the first sword-from-the-stone becoming broken ("you have broken what could not be broken—hope is broken") in a fight with Lancelot (upon their initial meeting) only to be accepted back, repaired and returned to Arthur by the "Lady of the Lake."

Other magical swords and spears appear in lore directly from a faction of Dragon Kings known in Celtic history as Tuatha d'Anu[*] (or "Tuatha de Dannan")—a group that first emerged from the Mesopotamian/Mediterranean region, migrating across the Danube and Rhine River Valleys through mainland Europe. Known elsewhere also as Andites ("Children of Andon"), Scythians (Sum-Aryans), Carpatheans, Dravidians, and other emerging cultures across Eurasia—high minds that blended with indigenous European populations, such as the La Tene culture classically represented in Celtic art styles. Until the populous rise of the Milesians (and then the Romans), the "Danubian Race" once *dominated* most of Europe.

THE "DANUBIAN" RACES OF EURASIA

• Dragons of Ireland retained the red hair, green eyes and fair or orange skin.
• Blue Race of Faerie retained the blond hair, blue (or silver) eyes and fair skin.
• Elven Race of Europe retained dark hair, dark eyes and fair (albinic) skin.

---

[*] See also the original *Mardukite Liber-D* discourse, released popularly as *"Book of Elven-Faerie"* by Joshua Free.

As relayed in our original *Mardukite Liber-D* discourse—survival and preservation of the "Dragon Legacy" in Europe was mainly a "genetic" act. We can see its significance in regards to cultural nationalism, but even this may stem from a deeper ingrained level of programming.

During the early inception of human civilization (and mass-social consciousness), we see many early covert efforts to fix a powerful "memory" in place, connected to *Anunnaki*—or "anunagi" *Star-Dragons*—and applied to the mass consciousness of the population, representing—at the very least—the "leading" members of the same population. During the *Dark Ages*, the Roman Church combated the "Dragon Legacy" with sweeping genocide and intellectual annihilation—such as we had never been seen before. As a result, the Dragon Kings and those with any claims to a pre-Christian legacy were no longer allowed to assume—or even be recognized for—their original and intended positions of world power: as humanity's guardians and earth stewards. Those remnants and shreds not blatantly destroyed by the Church turned underground for posterity—into the newly forming cabals and "secret societies" that have ever since captivated the imagination of the "surface world."

DEᴄIPhERIⱧ₲ ᴛhE DRⱯ₲ᴏⱧ
—ᴢYmᏰᴏLᴢ ᴏ৷ PᴏWER—

Symbols of the *Dragon*—or Dragon Power—appear at the root of all global mythologies, worldly systems and even religious or mystical beliefs. Dragons represent the cardinal or fundamental base icon of the creation and manifestation that we see in the cosmos, but also the "shadow" side of reality—the parts we do not readily see, what is not overtly apparent to human eyes. Regardless of where it appears, whether in contemporary spirituality or the esoteric practices of secret cabals and magical orders (organizations), the "Dragon Legacy" is the ultimate storehouse of infinite universal energy, cosmic power and perfect knowledge—and for this reason all of its purest aspects remain among the most closely guarded aspects of the Ancient Mystery Tradition. Elements of its use, true understanding of its lore, the "divine right" to enact its power on earth—all these things are generally reserved for the "highest degrees" and most "inner circles" of underground society.

Thousands of years of fear and misinformation enshroud the many facets of *Dragon Power*—enough so that the real topic has been kept out of the casual reach of most *Seekers*. That being said: there are certainly many references and allegories of true "dragon magic" and currents of "dragon energy" running rampant throughout the "New Age," but a true and faithful emphasis on its wide-sweeping implication is seldom found among them. Original interpretations of "dragon magic" reflect its energy as a raw and primordial force beyond individual "fragmented" understanding long before the more recent incorporation of this "cosmic dragon energy" as bands or rays of light—aspects or tears of manifestation that we can actually recognize easily and incorporate into mystical work.

While a *Seeker* may have been shown evidence for any number of ways of examining the existence and role of the Dragon—and what it represents in the histories of the surface world in contrast to its covert legacy—the "practical" magician, wizard or priestess will be at once moved to examine this subject on a completely different "level" within the domain of pragmatic mysticism. Within the confines of 'her' underground caverns or 'his' residence in some upper tower, the occult "Dragon-master" is prone to encountering Dragon Power as a highly tuned or refined "energetic" and "spiritual" quality that may be brought to a ritual or ceremonial level. Whether these rites are conducted in a physical "circle" or "temple," or are rather preferably operated strictly on the "astral plane," is another matter altogether. But for obvious reasons, blatant suggestion for "practical dragon magic" is reserved for the remainder of this collective treasury—*Draconomicon*—after having had first provided sufficient background material in former chapters. No doubt it is the more "obvious" applications of the *Dragon*, such as those popularly revived in modern or contemporary "New Age" approaches to *ritual magic*, that brings many readers to the pages of this book.

The symbolic "glyphs" of *Dragon Power* appearing within this current version of the *Draconomicon* are photographic reproductions from the 1990's "Merlyn Stone" edition, under the section heading: "Dracorum Grimoirum"—later excerpted for use by the Elven Fellowship Circle of Magick (EFCOM), an extension of the ("Mystics of the Earth/Draconis Celtic Lodge of Druids") that operated in the Rocky Mountains until 2001. It is the belief of the current editor that much of the source material circulated for decades in the underground before serving to structure other popular versions of modern "dragon magick" that emerged throughout the 1990's until today.

Deciphering the "symbols" themselves is actually quite easy if the seeker will at first remove the "blinders" of however many previous ways these "mysteries" have been approached. Concerning matters of true Dragon Power, we are dealing with the rawest state of creative energies in the universe—ones that later magicians, priestesses and sorcerers had to "filter" or "dilute" into more "accessible" or "useful" currents of power for their mystical rites, meditations and ritual operations. In this light, at its essence, primordial "dragon magic" is perhaps one of the most ancient and powerful esoteric traditions, if not the original archetypal paradigm that supports and validates its myriad of interpretative forms.

We recognize specific iconic symbols or pattern themes making repeated appearance in esoteric Dragon lore—and not only those examples within the *Draconomicon*, nor are these glyphs the only applicable examples for a "Dragonmaster" to use. The ones appearing here selectively represent a specific tradition, elsewhere we have branded "Pheryllt" or even "Mardukite" in our own revival systemology. Certainly, once a seeker is able to determine the nature of these fundamental or archetypal "root" aspects, the incorporation or "alchemical combination" of them for later use will be a simple exercise. Symbols only have "meaning"—and therefore, "power"—when the Seeker possesses full awareness and understanding of exactly what and why a "glyphs" is used. Otherwise, the practice of "magick" would be reduced to a series of *silly symbols* and *funny words* without meaning or purpose, and thus no end result.

Patterns found within the *"Dragon Glyphs"* may be interpreted based on one or more of the following motifs:

MOTIF PATTERNS IN DRAGON POWER SYMBOLS

1. The CIRCLE or "O" (omega)
2. The CROSS or "T" (tau)
3. "S" or "spiral" (waveform or curlicue)
4. A CIRCLE + CROSS (Celtic style or ankh)
5. A CIRCLE + CROSS (swastika)
6. A TRIANGLE or PYRAMID (delta)
7. Double "bars" (on ankh or cross)

THE CIRCLE – Representative of the *usumgal* or "Great Cosmic Dragon," the "circle" generally symbolizes *all* universal existence as one. The *ouroborus* serpent-circle is unique in that it is an unending shape with no actual "sides," and as such, has a relationship with "infinity"—or rather, the "illusion of infinity." It is only as a result of intellectual convenience coupled with the Mesopotamian religious system that humans quantified a circle divided by 360-degrees. In some cases, the circle— "O" *("oh")* or *omega*—is indicative of a "Gate," either all the "gates of the universe" as one or a literal "Gate to the Universe." In some traditions, this is the "Gate to the Outside," which separates the primordial "Abyss" (immaterial) from the primeval "Body of the Dragon" (material world) as alluded to in antiquated lore. Perhaps more 'Freudianesque' interpretations of the "circle" or "O" could lead seekers to consider more "sexual" symbolism, such as the open mouth, the womb and of course, the vagina. Naturally, the circle carries a feminine polarity, often indicative of the "water element" and in some applications, the "earth element."

THE CROSS – Long before its popular incorporation into Christianity—whether an equilateral "cross" ("+") or the "T" *("tee")* *tau*—the cross-sign may be found in our most ancient sources, symbolizing "cosmic power" as realized visibly in the physical (material) universe. The "equilateral cross" represents fragmentation of material existence into traditional "quarters," and when superimposed over the circle proper—Absolute Law spreading across infinity. In alchemy, the same symbol represents *salt*. In traditional occultism and indigenous shamanism, the four-armed cross often reflects "four winds" or "four directions" associated with *space* and the "air element." When compared to ancient Dragon lore from *Anunnaki* tablets, it can literally mean "crossings," such as "crossing of the heavens" or "crossing through the veils" (e.g. *"Crossing to the Abyss"*). On cuneiform tablet records, each Anunnaki proper name follows a determinative "AN" ("star-cross"-sign)—the origins for the *asterisk* symbol—and it is used three times ("MUL") to denote the name of a constellation or distant star.

THE "S"-CURVE or SPIRAL – Often resembling a "fancy" letter "*S*," spiral-like *curlicue* symbols or *wave-form* arcs appear in esoteric art, spiritual glyphs and "sigils" connected to Dragons and perhaps literally representative of the "serpent." The "*serpent*-coil" is almost always equated to Dragons, particularly the *Anunnaki* dragon-figures that were written into our histories as "engineers" of modern humans by affecting DNA, generally represented by wave-form patterns or intertwined serpents—the same intertwined serpents that are found in relation to the "T" (*tau*) or "tree" for the iconic "*serpent-staff*" or "serpent of wisdom" wrapped about the "tree of knowledge." We see the *caduceus* sign used even today in the medical field, leading us to the subject of our next symbol:

THE CIRCLE + CROSS (OT) *or* ANKH – Most famously depicted in Egyptian esoteric art, the *ankh* is notorious among New Age revivals as a symbol of "life." It actually evolved from the "S+ T" symbolism (described above), but it is categorized as the "circle and cross" or ("O+T") in part, due to the visible portion of the serpent's body forming an *omega* "O" above the "T" bar. When we consider the raw symbolism, it is identical to the serpent-coil of cosmic wisdom—the genetic (DNA) memory—encoded on and within all life—hence the programmable faculty of all life. The *ankh* ("O+T") is an "active" sign of Dragon energy, the application or use of "Will" ("Self") as a sentient active identity in existence—the "I-AM" or *Observer*.

In contrast, the "serpent around the tree" ("S+T") encompasses the whole field or parameter of potential energetic manifestation, such as is hidden beneath the surface of all existence. Traditional esoteric lore depicts the serpent-path of knowledge wrapped around and through the archetypal "*Tree of Life/Cosmos*"—such as we find in the Judaic *Kabbalah*. It is strikingly interesting by comparison that the most ancient Mesopotamian language identifies the "universe" as "AN-KI"—combined words for "heaven" and "earth," or the conjunction of seen and unseen aspects, above and below material existence, *All-as*-One.

THE CIRCLE + CROSS: "CELTIC" – Even before Christianization of pagan Europe, the Celts already used their own version of a "cross," undoubtedly incorporated into the culture from prehistoric proto-Druid—possibly Pheryllt—traditions. The early missionaries and bishops used the preexisting "Celtic Cross" to their advantage during the age of Christian conversion. For the Druids, a "Celtic Cross"—elongated with a smaller circle perfectly centered over its intersecting point—represented mystic *authority* and *mastery* over the "elemental kingdom," which on a celestial level is to include the whole of the cosmos or "physical universe." This is exactly the type of "True Authority" alluded to in Druidic lore, playing particularly high importance in the the current quasi-Pheryllt or neo-Pheryllt materials available to *Seekers* today.

THE CIRCLE + CROSS: "VAMPYRE'S SWASTIKA" – Famously corrupted by the Third Reich in Germany, the *swastika* is actually a positive Dragon power symbol used in diverse cultures throughout history to denote "divine radiance." Symbolically, it embodies a unique combination of all previously discussed icons, but in this particular form it represents the condensation and compression—the localized focus and dispersion—of cosmic dragon energy. One might even consider the energetic and allegorical connection to an "atomic bomb."

The use of it by the Nazi party was well researched; not an arbitrary choice. The same group utilized many versions of it, some more recognizably employing repetitive Nordic *sowelu* or "S" *runes*—those resembling a lightning bolt—representing the same "S" symbolism described prior. And, naturally, they understood it from within their own occult lodges to represent the same: powerfully directed energy; the application of will; dominant authority—and these things now carry very negative connotations in mass consciousness. But, raw Dragon power is simply that—its potential cannot be reduced to such mundane terms as "good" or "bad." To do so would place false limitations on an otherwise arbitrary cosmic systemology. The decision to nourish or destroy is retained with the individual.

THE TRIANGLE, DELTA, PYRAMID *or* "DRAGON'S EYE" – Most commonly found in traditions connected specifically with the Dragon Legacy, we discover an obscure three-armed version of the "divine radiance" icon or *swastika* as the "Dragon's Eye" —a triangular glyph reminiscent of the "pyramid-like" structures raised by many of these ancient cultures. It assuredly, in every instance, represents Absolute Power of Cosmic Law as present in the cosmos and exercisable on earth. Triangular or pyramidal shapes or solids share a long-standing history with the ancient dragon energy currents.

The triangle is found at the core of many magical glyphs, and pyramid-like structures appear in many places—not only in Egypt. The "Dragon's Eye" is probably the best representative sign for the Dragon Legacy and specifically traditions inspired by Pheryllt Druids. Triangles are definitively indicative of the "fire element," and as such, the "*delta*" sign is frequently used in science and mathematics to denote "action" and "change." We see other versions of the *delta-swastika* in threefold patterns of Celtic art, such as the *triscale* or *triskelion*, which are obviously versions of the original "Dragon's Eye." Esoteric interpretation may be aligned to the crossed-circle, but in this instance, the classical vision of a four-fold universe is instead "thirded." Additional Dragon lore suggests that the "Dragon's Eye" also indicates brain-channel by which a Dragonmaster is connected to the Absolute—meaning the pineal gland and idea of the "third eye."

DOUBLE-BARRED CROSS – One of the more famous heraldic crosses in Medieval Europe—particularly the Western parts and France—was the *Cross of Loarraine* distinguished by "two bars" as opposed to the traditional "one." Not ironically, given recent topics, it was the French Free Person's rival symbolic answer to the *swastika* used by the Nazi party. But before even this, it was a preferred symbol of Joan of Arc, and earlier, the Knights Templar. In ancient Mesopotamia, it represented the Babylonian scribe-god of wisdom, Nabu, and his secret society of scribes responsible for the cuneiform legacy of Babylon.

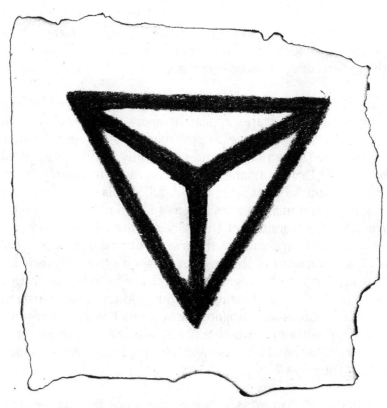

EYE OF THE DRAGON
—THE DRAGON'S EYE—

SWASTIKA OF THE VAMPYRE
—WHEEL OF THE DRAGON—

SERPENT ON THE TREE
OF KNOWLEDGE

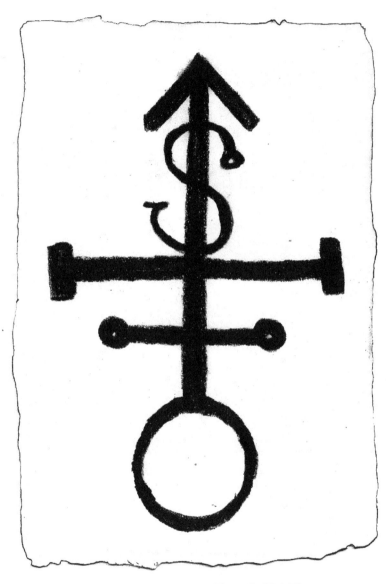

CROSS OF THE DRAGON
—DRAGON'S MIGHT—

BODY OF THE DRAGON
—DRAGON'S WILL—

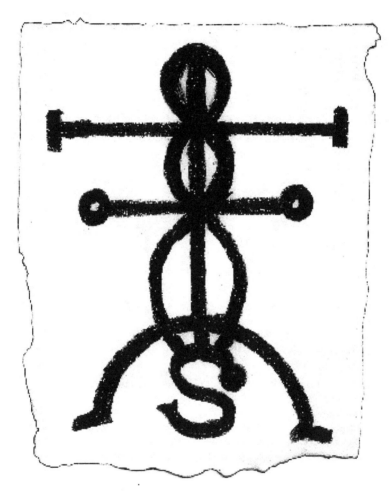

BREATH OF THE DRAGON
—DRAGON'S BREATH—

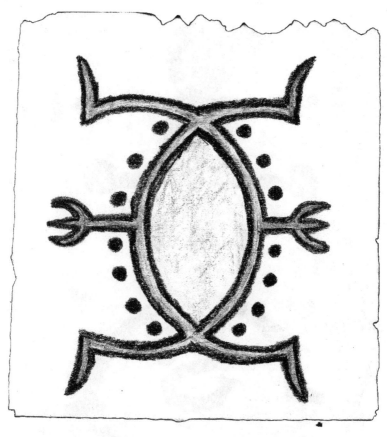

GATE OF THE DRAGON
—GATE TO THE ABYSS—

ƆhΛИИΣLIИ6 ThΣ DRΛ6DИ
—LIИΣƧ Dꞓ PDWER—

Our current volume demonstrates that Dragons represent the *actual* "power" directly feeding universal systems—certainly any worldly mystic understanding that might be revived from the Ancient Mystery School incorporates it. Thus far in our lessons, we have demonstrated many instances of Dragons appearing in esoteric lore, but very often the same "power" they represent seems almost intangible—an unseen driving force, very much like *electricity*. How appropriate that electromagnetic currents on the Earth planet—and a similar microcosmic energy system moving through the human organism—are literally interpreted as the "Power of the Dragon." For example, in some mystical texts, the Earth's outer surface energy grid of *electromagnetic* energy and other smaller *ley line* branches of the same are called "Dragon Lines." This is translated in the eastern schools as *kundalini*—a "dragon energy" that connects the life force of all creation, but which is specifically applied to practical "New Age" revivals of *chakra* lore, which are again referred to as "dragon currents" in the Pheryllt tradition.

The practice of "Dowsing" is probably one of the oldest pragmatic traditions connected to "channeling Dragon Lines" of the Earth planet. The method is famously used for locating underground water sources, finding missing objects, and most importantly for our purposes, *dowsing* or "divining" locations and pathways of *Ley Lines*. Metaphysically, "dowsing" is a form of *"radiethesia"*—involving electrical signals sent between the brain and muscles—operating by the same principles as pendulum divination. Experience may be earned through practice as many other occult skills, while the Dragonmaster learns to differentiate acts of muscle memory from real energy testing.

This form of magic requires the use of special "wands" called frequently "dowsing rods" or "dragon rods." Traditional natural versions of these wands are made from either a hazel or willow branch—one specifically selected that forms a natural "Y." According to lore, it is preferable if the tree it is taken from grows near a natural source of water. These "Y-types" are the original "forked-form" of the *rod*, gripped by the ends of two "legs." With shoulders relaxed and elbows at the sides of the body, the central stem extends outward in front of the operator.

Another version of the Dragon Rods also appear in Pheryllt lore—the "L-type"—popularly revived today. This method actually requires a set of two "L-shaped rods" each held in the same manner just described, apart from one another in each hand. Modern "L-rods" are constructed from either bent or fabricated metal, usually copper. Modern innovators have even used pieces from wire coat-hangers cut with a long arm and a relatively shorter base bent at a 90-degree angle to the arm—so as to form a capital letter "L" shape, hence the name. The base-handle should be wrapped in cardboard or a drilled out length of dowel that allows the arms to swing freely when held. Beginners may choose to craft them from a loose cardboard tube-wrap, since this method can also be combined with muscle-tensing energy-testing exercises. In either case, when the specific energy frequency (or object) visualized (and projected from the mind) has been reached, "Y-stem" wands drop downward and the "L-style" swing inward towards each other or crossing over each other (depending on how they are held).

The mind emits a particular vibration relative to its focus—an important key to remember when holding any visualization or emotionally-charged imagery in the "mind's eye." When used in practical "energy work" or methods of dowsing, a specific frequency is maintained in this manner until it becomes noticeably stronger by constructively interfering with a similar current of energy. This can be felt through muscular tensing, involuntary reactions to energy, caused by internal impulses.

With some skill and practice, practitioners can also use dowsing rods to "test" or "measure" the boundaries and strength of energy fields, like auras and *ley lines*. Once these methods are mastered, the same principles could be applied to even more specific examples of energy work—it simply requires repeated experience and memory of the "sense" related to each type of energy encountered, just as you naturally have learned to associate and identify with different "colors" and "sounds" and "smells," &tc.

Although tools can respond differently with different operators, the "L-rods" have a tendency to swing outward, not in, when encountering radiant energy like an aura around a person, but this is not an absolute rule, especially if a practitioner has already programmed themselves and their use of tools to respond otherwise. With free movement in two directions on this axis, "yes/no" answers can be determined in the same way that fluxing energy is measured. Therefore, a practitioner might program an in-ward swing (of "L-rods") or downward arc (of "Y-wands") to display either positive or negative energy flows—and we are speaking in purely amoral terms here concerning positive and negative or the polarity of projective and receptive aspects of energetic movement. An experienced Dragonmaster develops natural sensitivity to energy because of their constant conscious interaction with universal forces— as a result many learn how to even use their own "muscular inclinations" (without the aid of tools) to "test" energies.

* * *

Energy work associated with what is called Chakra and Kundalini lore in the East is mirrored in the Pheryllt Druid spiritual doctrines of CALEN—the *prana* of the East or the *astyr* or Starcenters of Moroii ad Vitam Dragon Tradition—light-centers of life-force, a personal energetic distribution system within all living creatures. The more commonly used word—*chakra*—is derived from the Sanskrit language, meaning "*wheel.*" They are described such because they act like "fan-blades" or "turbines," continually gathering a projecting a particular current or vibration of "dragon current" or "ray of light"—as it is perceived in the realm of "forms," which is also to say the "realm of lights." The activity of this projected energy creates an "energetic field" around the body—a "light shield" in Pheryllt lore or *astra* in the modern Moroii ad Vitam revival tradition—the electromagnetic field generally called the "aura." As explained in the teachings of Moroii ad Vitam "Book of V"—

> "*Astyr* each have their own facets, properties and sub-systems, which we simply call their *function*. We continuously process *Starfyre*—and *astyr* are the processing machines. They function together as a system. Like interlocking gears, they are not truly separate from one another.

> "*Astra*—The Luminous Body—often called the *aura* by many New Age practitioners—is the result of radiation from the energy cycling processes of the *astyr*. Any energy that you come into contact with is being pulled in, processed and then projected out through *astyr*.

> "As new energy flows into the system, other processed energy flows out, like water running through a household pipe. As you use it, drawing it out, water fills in from the Source to replace it. And much like a water-wheel, innate faculties exist to circulate *Starfyre* through our system."

"Calen" (*chakras, astyr, &tc.*) are an energetic link between the metaphysical "mind-spirit" and the physical body. Together with the "aura"/"astra" this personal energy system contributes to who you are (personality), how you feel (emotion) and whatever others feel or perceive from you (persona). Each individual light center operates with a specific dragon current. The projected vibrations you come into contact with from your external environment--via transference and resonance—also get perceived and processed through the appropriate "Calen" filter.

Each "type" of energy—and its corresponding "filter-wheel"—is concentrated in a specific relative position within the body.

Your "lower" faculties, connecting to your lower animal survival-driven self, exists relatively "low" on the body (below the heart). By comparison, "higher" faculties (most often attributed to a higher self) are all processed closer to (and including) your head. Auric emanations are typically stronger in the "higher" regions of spiritually-minded seekers, which can sometimes make them more susceptible to "distractions of the lower" if these centers go "unchecked" or "unbalanced."

Maintaining and balancing the entire "chakra system" does not require advanced and obscure rituals or ceremonial observations. Awareness and consciousness—the use of will and intention—sufficiently manifests personal energetic change. When someone's "aura" is dim or fragmented—or they say "they feel drained" or have "no energy"---their *chakras* are not functioning at proper frequency and amplitude. There is *no* shortage of energy in existence, but static energy and restrictive blockages cause resistance to a natural flow. Since the "chakras" are frequencies related to color (or light rays), many esoteric sources suggest that colored stones, crystals, filtered light and/or fabric squares (&tc.) can all be used as focal aids for this type of work.

"*Chakras*" function automatically—but until you actually look inward to "see" and be *aware* of them, they are not fully in your range of control. It is only when the Observer *observes* that there is conscious interaction between. Beyond that, it is a matter of visualization and willpower. Maintaining control is important because free and healthy action of this system is what contributes to a healthy and vibrant "aura," just as electrical currents create magnetic fields as a result of their activity and intensity. The "*astra field*" or "aura" is the part of you that radiates into the space around you and does the energetic "feeling"—like your skin provides for the body. It is the part that interacts with all *fields* subjectively considered "outside" of the "I" or Self. Although nothing is separate, mental attentions affect how you feel and experience existence and also affects how others "feel" when they are around you.

The following reveals basic descriptions of the *Dragon currents* as they relate to the *personal energy system* otherwise called "*Calen*," "*chakras*" or "*astyr*." Obviously variations exist in New Age revivals regarding the sequencing and classification of these "light centers." This list provided follows the consensus found throughout the current author's collected works:—

"CALEN" – INNER STARFIRE -or- THE DRAGON WITHIN

1.

Base or Root: located at the base of the spine (or feet), and controls basic survival instincts, the wild/animal nature and physical ability required to exist and function. Colors: Ascension = white, Elven = green; use red (if underactive) or green (if overactive). Stones: [green] Amazonite, aventurine, emerald and moss agate.

2.

Sacral or spleen: located just above the penis or between the ovaries, and controls sexual reproduction and carnal pleasure. Colors: Ascension = violet, Elven = blue; use orange (if underactive) or blue (if overactive). Stones: [blue] Hematite, lapis lazuli, pearl and topaz.

3.

Solar plexus: located near the stomach, and controls digestive, emotional and ritualistic faculties. Colors: Ascension = purple (and gold), Elven = red; use yellow (if underactive) or purple (if overactive). Stones: [red] Agate (red), jasper (red), and ruby.

4.

Heart or Merkaba: located near the heart, and controls the circulatory system, balance of the other rays and personal healing faculties. Colors: Ascension = pink, Elven = purple (and pink); use green (if underactive) or pink (if overactive). Stones: [purple and blue] Rose quartz, quartz, sapphire and turquoise.

5.

Throat: located at the throat near the thyroid, and controls communication, speech, some telepathy and voice. Colors: Ascension = blue, Elven = orange; use blue (if underactive) or orange (if overactive). Stones: [orange] Amber, carnelian, jacinth and opal.

6.

Third Eye or brow: located near the pineal gland, and controls the endocrine system, immunity, personal magnetism, imagination and visualization. Colors: Ascension = green, Elven = yellow; use indigo (if underactive) or soft orange/ yellow (if overactive). Stones: [yellow] Diamond, gold, tiger's eye and topaz.

7.

Crown or Flower of Life: located just above the head, and controls our spiritual and metaphysical interconnectedness, the subconscious mind and the use of intention. Colors: Ascension = yellow, Elven = violet; use violet (if underactive) or yellow (if overactive). Stones: [violet] Primarily amethyst quartz.

Fields such as the *astra* or *aura* are often described as *"spherical."* They do radiate or cycle outwardly from a central point— *Calen,* the *chakras,* or *astyr.* But, since there is more than one central point involved in this system, the *field* is more elliptical or egg-shaped when incorporating all present energies that generally run up the spinal region.

Dragonmasters also perform magic by *calling forth* (or "evoking") *Starfyre Radiance* from the "Source" or the "*Great Cosmic Dragon*" using *Awareness, Will, Intention* and *Emotion.* Modern practitioners find that identifying the *Rays* by color is a most convenient and accurate way of differentiating their relative degrees on a continuous "spectrum." The color—and thereby, nature—of one's own "Light Shield" or "aura" may even be altered to match and attract the energy currents desired.

Dragonmasters can call the energy down like a beam of light from the stars. You can experiment with this using visualization and will, allowing yourself to absorb and radiate energy specific to a particular "center" or you can work through the series of them to make sure the whole system is operating at optimum performance. Following the standards of the Dragon Tradition popular to the Druids and Pheryllt Dragon Order, the Singular Force is divided by the Three Divine Rays of Awen —being "silver," "crystalline" and "golden." These in turn are divided, fragmented or condensed into a spectrum of seven bands of light—matching the same *Dragon currents* that form the basis of reality.

THE SILVER (LEFT) RAY

Sound/Letter: I ("*ee*")
Polarity: Female, dark, passive, lunar.
Quartile Element: Water (some Earth)
Elvish Element: The Sea
Physical Manifestation: The Mineral Kingdom
Threshold Time Period: Dusk, sunset, autumn.
Elessar (Elf-Stone): Silver (hematite)
Light Bands (Rays): Indigo, violet and blue.

The Silver Properties of the Light Rays
VIOLET (Saturn): Astral vision, darkness,
      Otherworld work, wisdom, wards.
      Domain: Element of Vapor/Cloud
INDIGO (Jupiter): Beauty, enchantment,
      emotions, love, music, play.
      Domain: Element of Rain
BLUE (Luna): Compassion, dreams, healing,
      peace and understanding.
      Domain: Element of Sea

THE GOLD (RIGHT) RAY

Sound/Letter: O ("*oh*")
Polarity: Masculine, light, active, solar.
Quartile Element: Fire and Air
Elvish Element: The Sky
Phys. Manifestation: Animal & Human Kingdoms
Threshold Time: Dawn, sunrise, spring/summer.
Elessar (Elf-Stone): Gold (tiger's eye)
Light Bands (Rays): Yellow, orange and red.

The Golden Properties of the Light Rays
YELLOW (the Sun): Knowledge, intellect,
    confidence, and inspiration.
    Domain: Element of Skyfire
ORANGE (Mercury): Communication, courage,
    being aware, wishes.
    Domain: Element of Star
RED (Mars): Transformation, healing, strength,
    willpower, and leadership.
    Domain: Element of Flame

THE CRYSTALLINE (MIDDLE) RAY

Sound/Letter: A ("*ah*")
Polarity: Neutral, crystalline, reflective
Quartile Element: Earth ('Quintessence.')
Elvish Element: The Land
Physical Manifestation: Plant & Tree Kingdom
Threshold Time: Twilight, midnight, winter.
Elessar (Elf-Stone): Black (obsidian) or Green
Light Band (Ray): Green

The Crystalline Properties of the Light Ray
GREEN (Venus): Life-force, balance, healing,
    growth, true love.
    Domain: Element of Earth

Cosmic Dragon Energy—sometimes called *Starfyre*—flows fluid like *water*; it burns and transforms like *fire*; it permeates in all spaces of *air*, and can condense to a slow vibration solidifying like *earth*. Eastern traditions refer to this "element" as the quintessential state of *Akasha*—the *"Fifth Element."*

Potential use of this information is literally only limited to the extent of imagination driven WILL—a combination of the ability to BE and the ability to DO. It is certainly not restricted to any specific semantics, paradigm or suggestion by the current author and/or this book.

ƧUMMﬨﬨING ThE DRAGﬨN
—ﬨAƧTING AﬨD ﬨﬨﬨJURIﬨG—

It is apparent—especially considering the "American Infesta-tion" of the Dragon—that modern "New Age" *Dragon Magic* and elements of "fantasy," found in both popular culture and sub-cultural themes, share a mutually contributory relationship with one another. Any boundary line between purely arcane esoteric occultism and purely imaginative fantasy-media en-tertainment began to definitively blur at least fifty years ago. Several overlapping examples of arcane lore and fantasy even appear within the pages of our *Draconomicon*—where we note that in the fantasy roleplaying game "Dungeons and Dragons," scepters and artifacts made from gold and rubies attract and call dragon energy—and this rings true. The Latin incantation appearing in the motion picture, *"Dragonslayer,"* or the Gaelic "Charm of Making" from *"Excalibur,"* are also found among the practical magic suggestions from "21 Lessons of Merlyn"— and we have already provided a treatment on these examples within our current "grimoire" tome dedicated to the Dragon.

Furthermore, it is both dangerous and ignorant to either dis-regard or blindly accept any material or suggestion of lore simply because of where it may appear. A true Dragonmaster applies *discernment* in every way, to every thought and before every intentional act. The fact that some piece of widely avail-able—or even not so well known—information should appear simultaneously in esoteric/occult literature and fantasy media productions and games, is not in itself an indicator or validat-ing quality of anything other than: the world is really quite small, data exchanges hands easily, inspiration is around every corner, in every book, and we have no way of knowing how covertly connected or informed these creators are.

Corresponding with the mid-1990's, while the current author was first investigating the nature of the *Pheryllt* and specifically the presence of the *Dragon* in the "New Age" movement, several others appeared to be doing the same on their own paths, all of which were tapping into the same basic cosmic energy stream in their own way. For example, one New Age author, *D.J. Conway* spent considerable energy bringing the surface lore of the Dragon to the wiccan and other neopagan communities. Her *Dragon Tradition* is specifically recognizable for its alignment with her supporting literary contributions— much like our *Draconomicon* is in serial with a greater Druidic and "Mardukite" literary collection by its author. Regardless, it has become quite influential on popular New Age traditions.

Most popular "New Age" traditions are deemed "surface lore." The materials are not meant for the truly esoteric practitioner or occult initiate and are instead the shreds and tears poured out for mainstream publication—even if presented mysterious and "occult." That being said, there are many of us in the underground that still find these "surface world" publications interesting and/or inspirational—but they do not generally reflect the deeper "underground" stream of esoteric lore that has been present "beneath-the-surface" of human existence for thousands of years since the first records of Mesopotamia. There are certainly many allusions to a time even before this, but it is the verifiable literary continuum of human history that the current author's "esoteric library" is drawn from.

In the instance of "surface lore," we find a paradigm that most New Age practitioners are familiar with and can assimilate into any practice and tradition—a paradigm of "elemental magick" with a glossy dragon patina. Elemental Dragon Magick or "Dragon Alchemy" involves the same correspondences used in traditional "ritual magic" (or ceremonial magick). Perhaps one of the only key differences is the manner of creating the nemeton—or sacred ritual space—and attribution of elemental domains ("realms" or "kingdoms") to the reigning Elemental Dragon Guardians of the "Five Rings" tradition.

TRADITIONAL NEW AGE ELEMENTAL DRAGON GUARDIANS

SAIRYS – Dragon of Air; eastern quadrangle
FAFNIR – Dragon of Fire; southern quadrangle
NAELYAN – Dragon of Water; western quadrangle
GRAEL – Dragon of Earth; northern quadrangle

Dragons are called, summoned and even alchemically formed by Druids, priestesses and Dragon-mages conducting magic on the *astral plane*. Occasionally, the Dragonmaster may seek to call dragon energy to concentrate in a physical locale, ritual circle, or to internally invoke its nature and qualities. There is no shortage of ritual correspondences that can be applied. Using traditional names to "call the quarters" or imbue popular steps of ceremony: *air* for preparing the incense; *fire* for lighting it; alchemical union of salt (*earth*) in *water*, &tc. Whatever course chosen, the *nemeton* must be made receptive to vibrate desired "dragon currents" of energy. To do so, the practitioner raises energy aligned with a "ray of light" corresponding to the fire element. Eventually you can combine any element or combination of elements specific to the alchemical "type" of dragon energy you are calling—hence *"Dragon Alchemy."*

Numerous pages could be filled relaying beautifully composed rhymes and poetry with names and actions for ritual use. It is more effective when a practitioner writes them out or articulates their own intentions personally. Basic premises are the same: to attract any draconic energy, you must first attune your internal and external environment to align with and attract dragon-friendly vibrations. This may be achieved via use of an esoteric exercise called the "Dragon's Breath." A similar practice appears in most traditions of "dragon magic," making this practicum the perfect preliminary to all forms of energy work pertaining to the Dragon, and ritual styles that incorporate dragon energy. Numerous variations may be drawn from basic formulas and suggestions throughout our current tome.

THE RITE OF THE DRAGON'S BREATH

When the nemeton is prepared for energy work, begin "quad-breathing" or "fire-breathing"—the rhythm of breathing in for *four counts* and exhaling for *four counts*. [Too many differing opinions exist regarding "holding" any breaths, whether emptied or full.] Call down (summon forth) the fiery rays of dragon energy that you can visualize—feel and sense—all around you. As you inhale, take this radiant energy inside through your breath and every pore of your body. Continue to cycle these "pressures building" within of the "Dragon's Breath." Feel it stream throughout your entire body, emanating into and out of your aura, charging the space occupying the nemeton and ambient surrounding environment. If you so choose, you may even combine an incantation with your gauged "dragon breath" exhalation into the air around you. The suggested selection, of course, being the *Charm of Making*:—

anail nathair (*anail nathrack*)
orth'bhais's bethad (*ortha bhais-is beatha*)
do cheal deanaimh (*do chel denmha*)

"Dragon Calling" may effectively rate temperatures of the ambient space in the *nemeton*. Buildup of fire energy in the body for the "Dragon's Breath" may also raise the body's personal temperature, a sensation that can actually be uncomfortable for some practitioners. Traditionally faerie lore suggests that iron is anathema to fey, yet mystical sources generally agree that its energy is aligned specifically with the Dragon. Iron correlates to the both fire element and Mars planet in traditional alchemy, making it a suitable attractant for specifically draconic energies. Another popular attractant is "Dragon's Blood" essence, which can be present in ritual as a stone or an incense.

Blood and Breath are critical components of true "Dragon magic"—and are even classified as the core ingredients of all magic in the Moroii ad Vitam Dragon tradition. The idea of Dragon's Breath roots back to Mesopotamia and the "Breath of Life" given to human beings by the "creators," which was first drawn out of the *Primeval Dragon* or First Cause—the LAW. Another reference to "Dragon's Blood" is made regarding the genetic component of Dragon Kings, mystics, priestesses and, of course, the proverbial Dragon Priests, the *Pheryllt*. It is now assumed this component or essence may be substituted with the palm-resin carrying the same name: "Dragon's Blood."

Any of the symbols or glyphs found in the *Draconomicon* are appropriate for rituals, meditation and energy work. The one that probably has the longest standing history in connection to *Dragon Magic* is the "Dragon's Eye" This ancient sigil can be traced on the ground with a sword—or ceremonial representation of a sword—or fire elemental weapon sacred to Dragons. Rather then defer to derivatives, it is most appropriate to include the original basic outline of the *Rite of Dragoncall* here, as excerpted from modern Pheryllt tradition.

THE RITE OF DRAGONCALL

Performance Suggestions: Incorporate as many Dragon energy attractants into your ritual as possible. Consider all correspondences to the sun, fire element, the planet Mars, gold and iron metals, &tc. The threshold time and natural terrain should be appropriate to the element of the Dragon energy called—typically fire: thus, high noon or dawn; the summer season; mountains, hills and caves. Some lore suggests the Dragonmasters wear a red cloak or robe with a golden "Dragon's Eye on the back for ceremonial purposes. Ritual practices may be as dramatic (external) or astral oriented (internal) as needed. You may use a ceremonial sword—or wooden representation when applicable—or you may choose to use no physical tools if necessary or required. The original formula is written for use with a sword. Some of the ceremonial Dragon swords are not meant for practical warfare—some are not even sharpened. A wooden sword or staff can be fashioned, carved and decorated to serve the same purpose. You may employ the Evocation of the Dragon in combination with any preferred Dragon names from any applicable language, so long as they are personally significant to you.

• Cast a circle of 12 stones high on a hillside, mountain region or cave and prepare the nemeton properly.

• With the sword—or representation—trace the symbol of the "Dragon's Eye" in the center of the circle.

• Consecrate the charcoal and "Dragon's Blood" resin. Then light it.

• Summon the "Dragon's Breath."

• Raise the sword—pointed high into the air—as you thrice intone your names and evocations of the Dragon:

Draco. Draco. Draco. Draig. Draig. Draig.
Draconis. Draconis. Draconis. Vovim. Vovim. Vovim.
Evo - He - Oi Ia Salman ca Vovim.
Hear the words of the Dragonmaster in the Old Tongue:
Cum saxum saxorum,
In a duresum montum operaum da
in aet lutum inquinatum, Draconis!

• In one swift action and exhalation, plunge the sword deep into the earth.

• Seat yourself in the center of the "Dragon's Eye" and continue Dragon magic, meditation or energy work.

• Remove the sword at the end of the rite.

2IST CENTURY DRAGONS
—A MODERN INFESTATION—

Ever since our first glimpses of iconic imagery and lore from ancient Mesopotamia, the Dragon has always remained something of an enigma in human consciousness. Once restricted to a realm of fantasy, demonology or distant inconsequential mythologies, we have witnessed a progressive reemergence of the Dragon in mystical and metaphysical revivals of the past century. It represents one primary avenue back to the distant sources of esoteric knowledge—the type coveted today in this New Age "information era." It represents a shifting of the age —an awakening and unfolding of laden faculties as a call put forth by our planetary system to entrust stewardship to a generation of new Guardians. As a result—the Dragon presence has risen in modern consciousness, and subsequently popular modern culture and subculture.

When we consider the inception and rise of modern "fantasy" culture, one name unmistakeably stands apart—J.R.R. Tolkein. His "dragon" became popularly iconic, inspiring minds across several generations and perhaps even the contemporary literary domain of "epic fantasy." Although inspired by archetypal mythologies, Tolkein's "Middle Earth" prompted post-modern society to critically consider the need of a "cultural mythos." This is only loosely present in our Western civilization, which lends itself mainly to capitalist trends and dry hollow entertainment or media industry cash-grabs. Although absent from the "*Lord of the Rings*" literary trilogy itself, "*The Hobbit*" famously featured the dragon: Smaug. And for as long as it's been available—c. 1939—"*The Hobbit*" and its dragon have probably influenced more popular "epic fantasy"—including "*Dungeons and Dragons*"—than any other piece of "fantasy" media.

The 1960's brought an new era of "fantasy" and "psychedelic enchantment" all chock-full of wizards, unicorns and dragon themes. Consider the early Disney rendition of "*Sword-in-the-Stone*" where Madam Nim turns into a dragon during her wizards' duel with Merlyn the magician; or, in another of their films, "*Sleeping Beauty,*" a fey-female sorceress Maleficent also transforms into the form of a dragon at one juncture. But, the Dragon appears elsewhere in softer tones for our youth, and in these example, the Dragon is usually a friend—not some horrendous beast that we must destroy in fear. The song and film "*Puff the Magic Dragon*" seems to have inspired a certain segment of the past generations, a nostalgic staple for some, as timeless perhaps as "*Pete's Dragon*" and similar lovable classics are for others. And while no dragon blatantly appears, the same spirit and energy is found in Peter S. Beagle's classic— "*The Last Unicorn.*"

"Dungeons and Dragons"—D&D—is a fantasy role-playing tabletop game system developed by Gary Gygax in the 1960's. It first launched publicly in 1974 as a series of small kits and booklets from Gygax's own kitchen. By the time of D&D's public release, Gygax was an established game-developer. His first medieval fantasy "miniatures" tabletop war-game—Chainmail —inspired formation of his group, "Lake Geneva Tactical Studies Association" in Wisconsin. The group later rebranded to form an official publishing company: "Tactical Studies Rules," better known as TSR. The "Miniatures" battle games in many ways resembled more advanced variations on themes found in similar mainstream classics, such as "Risk." All TSR products emphasized practical use of game theory in theoretical "play" out of military tactics and battle strategy.

In 1977, TSR launched their first edition of "Advanced Dungeon & Dragons"—or AD&D—but what players would continue to simply call "D&D." This version of the game consisted of new expanded rules available in separate hardcover books— the "Core Rulebooks"—allowing for infinite expansion supplement possibilities, an aspect that TSR took full advantage of.

The core books required for the game are *"The Player's Hand-book," "Dungeon Master's Guide"* and the *"Monster Manual"*—all of which were originally written by Gary Gygax himself. This same model has continued to represent the game for 40 years, although the editions themselves have been consistently up-dated by other writers. In fact, even the original release of the AD&D Core saw revision within its first year after debut cover artwork was deemed too "demonic" and controversial, so a more commercial feel was brought to the same books in 1978. Further titles later supplemented the core materials, includ-ing: *"Deities & Demigods," "Manual of the Planes"* and widely controversial *"Fiend Folio."*

While building in popularity "Dungeons & Dragons" began to spark religious controversy almost immediately. Most were concerned about "devil-worship," but other strange things started happening to psychologically unstable teenagers ob-sessed with either the occult elements and/or the character "role-play" of the game. Certainly, these games obviously ex-pose players to metaphysical, fantasy and magical themes, but no more than an extremist personality might find exploring Grimm Faerie Tales and archaic mythologies. The one element these types of games do actually provide is a social community for those interested in these themes for any number of per-sonal reasons or inclinations—including practical occultism.

The first real bout of public concern emerged in 1979 when a young player attending the University of Michigan—James Dallas Egbert III—disappeared for nearly a month. As media attention developed, so did the story: the young man's reality irreversibly merged with the game world, so he went into the steam ducts of the university for personal adventure and died. None of this turned out to be true and sales skyrocketed. Later it was discovered that Egbert was simply missing due to his own psychological instability—but he did commit suicide a year later. Throughout the 1980's, it was commonplace for the news media to associate D&D with all manners of misdirected youth activity—satanism, cults, suicide or even murders.

Negative attention enshrouding the D&D brand in the early 1980's eventually did influence a noticeable decline of sales. Many executive shareholders for TSR decided to "get out." But Gary Gygax had faith in his vision, commissioning a Saturday-morning cartoon: "Dungeons & Dragons." It aired on CBS from September 1983 until November 1985, adjusting adult themes inherent in the game to provide a greater appeal to younger audiences. When the series released to DVD, it included a special gaming supplement allowing players to adapt elements and characters of the animated series into their tabletop play.

In 1989, TSR produced a new "Second Edition" of AD&D that corresponded with a complete revision of all rules and supplements. As the company struggled to manage ongoing financial problems, it sought to not only retain existing players, but to attract a whole new generation with a revitalized look and feel to the product. Yet, a decade later, TSR faced bankruptcy, and their design patents and trademarks were purchased by Wizards of the Coast—a company responsible for another widely successful quasi-occult fantasy game system called "*Magic: The Gathering*" or MTG. Wizards of the Coast went on to release a new streamlined version of D&D as a "Third Edition" in 2000—returning the game title to simply: Dungeons & Dragons. This debut of a new edition coincided with the first feature-length "*Dungeons & Dragons*" motion picture ever, followed by a sequel in 2005: "*Wrath of the Dragon God.*" [Wizards of the Coast has since been purchased by the Hasbro toy company, and as of 2020, the game system is currently in its "Fifth Edition."]

The "*Draconomicon*" also appears within the D&D game system, first released in relation to the "Forgotten Realms" campaign in 1990 to correspond with AD&D 2nd Edition rules. The work has reappeared in expanded forms for subsequent editions of the game—revised in 2003 for the 3rd Edition, then as a two volume set in 2008 and 2009 for the 4th Edition—Volume One: "*Chromatic Dragons*" and Volume Two: "*Metallic Dragons.*" As a person might guess, these rules supplements emphasize game lore and adventures related to all things "*dragon.*"

In August 2014, the inaugural 5th Edition D&D Epic Adventure sprawled across two hardcover volumes: "*Hoard of the Dragon Queen*" and "*The Rise of Tiamat.*" This serial—otherwise called "*Tyranny of Dragons*"—exploited three original D&D subcultural game staples: the "Sword Coast" (between Baldur's Gate and Icewind Dale) of "*Forgotten Realms*"; the iconic centralization of high fantasy adventure surrounding, literally, "Dungeons" and "Dragons"; and finally, themed emphasis toward primordial lore—albeit a fantasy interpretation—of the most famous dragon deity of D&D mythology... *Tiamat.*

Tiamat is present in the D&D franchise from its inception. As we should expect, she is not represented 'one-to-one' with the Mesopotamian mythos—yet there is little doubt that it served as inspiration for what is essentially the *most important* dragon in all of D&D. Tiamat is the patron dragon god—and perhaps primeval mother—for *all* the evil "Chromatic Dragons," those dragons distinguished by their colored hue of the fragmented rays of primordial creation: black, blue, green, red and white. Dragons of these types are "inherently evil" in the D&D game system—but they are not the only kinds that emerged from the *Astral Sea*. Another type: wiser, less bent toward greed and malice, took shape, balancing *cosmic draconian forces*—"Metallic Dragons"—brass, bronze, copper, gold, silver dragons, and those choosing to follow the ancient dragon god Bahamut, the "Platinum Dragon."

As relayed via D&D Cosmology, dragons are perhaps the oldest and most powerful manifestations in the cosmos—born from the primordial world, of primordial gods—shaped and formed from the rawest purest forms of cosmic energy. Of these primordial deities, the First Dragon or proto-Dragon appearing in lore is the Primordial God "IO"—the "Ninefold Dragon," "Concordant Dragon," "Swallower of Shades" and "Great Eternal Wheel." The god *Io* is the original creator of *Dragonkind*—as explained in the 4th Edition D&D *Draconomicon*: "creating mortal vessels that would not only live in the world of elements, but would give life and soul to the elements themselves."

This D&D "Epic of Creation" mirrors the historical Babylonian tablets in many respects: it takes place during a primordial era of cosmic development; it involves dragons or dragon-like gods, even a primary one among them with the ability to create expressions of life by infusing primary elemental energies with mortal simulacrum; and finally our "Epics" are always set beyond the material realm, at the furthest reaches of pure existence—spaces between the spaces we see in our condensed solidified experience. But, our similarities do not end there, to which we will refer to a small portion of the D&D narrative:—

"During the Dawn Wars between the 'primordials' and the gods that followed the world's creation, Io and his children stood at the forefront of all mortal beings in the fight to preserve creation from the unchecked elemental forces of the angry primordials. Io fought and defeated many primordials, but one of them, Erek Hus—the King of Terror—slew Io. Just when the primordials seemed on the verge of victory, from the halves of Io's shattered body, two new gods arose: Bahamut, the Platinum Dragon; and Tiamat, the Chromatic Dragon.

"Bahamut and Tiamat together defeated the King of Terror, but then Tiamat turned against the noble Bahamut, attempting to seize dominion as Queen of All Dragons—she could not suffer the existence of any equal or allow any other creature to reign over dragonkind. But, the Platinum Dragon defeated Tiamat, and she retreated to the dark depths of Tytherion, the *Endless Night* or *Abyss*."

Since the 1970's, the primeval Dragon Tiamat has carried this particular sheen in D&D culture. She is quite unique—as the archetypal "Chromatic Dragon"—manifesting as an immortal beast with not one, but *five* heads, one for each primary chromatic dragon color. She also has abilities to appear humanoid as a stunning "dark-haired female mage," but this creature is never able to be truly destroyed by heroes—"discorporating" back into the Nine Hells if mortally wounded or "bloodied."

In the "Tyranny of Dragons" campaign, heroes in town find themselves under attack by a powerful organization network of Tiamat worshipers—the "Cult of the Dragon." This ancient cult is dedicated to recovering five "Chromatic Dragon Masks" to combine with powerful rituals that will summon the dragon god Tiamat present into the physical realms—thereby annihilating material existence as we know it. Parallels with darker aligned "left-hand path" and "Typhonian" occult traditions, or even the quasi-mystical "Cthulhu Mythos," are too numerous and superfluous to our previous lessons to list here—but they are certainly recognizable by intermediate level *Seekers*.

Interests in collecting and "standardizing" fantasy lore—especially about *dragons*—erupted strongly in the 1980's. The D&D gaming system provided one option for this, establishing the benchmark to compare and interpret a consensus of all global mythologic, religious and supernatural elements in one place. What's more: it even provided relevant statistics of these facets. At the very least, the standard provided for an onslaught of increased mass awareness and media productions. We have made a long cultural journey since the days of *"Dragonslayer"* and *"Excalibur"* in the early 1980's. We are only now seeing the *"Harry Potter"* generation emerge into the world of adult systems, now experienced in tether to a long string of successful fantasy franchises—from *"Dragonheart"* in the mid-1990's to *"Eragon"* and, of course, the almost too perfect of an example: *"How to Train Your Dragon."* The potential list of examples is seemingly endless.

The subject of "dragon lore"—whether real or imagined—has developed into its own subcultural niche, evolving and growing for at least four decades publicly. The timeless pursuit is acknowledged simultaneously by adults and young people at their own levels. Several "Dragonology" titles have appeared on the market, reminiscent of the more mature presentation of "Verminology" in 1980 by Pamela Blanpied—in *"Dragons: A Guide to the Modern Infestation."* The work is presented academically as a zoologic and ethnographic report about dragons!

According to Pamela Blanpied's report, the academic research is derived from—an otherwise unknown—"The New Zealand School of Dragon Studies" (NZSDS). The country is primarily untouched and, probably by no small coincidence, has become the choicest environment for fantasy-genre filmmakers of our time. Even if a complete work of fiction, Blanpied correctly pinpoints a region on earth that is most likely to host real life dragon activity, safely remote and distanced from the human world. Depending on our application of dragon "semantics" as suggested throughout our lessons, a physical and perhaps inter-dimensional pursuit of "dragon phenomonology" might actually be quite valid. If we are to expand that semantic view a bit further, it is possible that we might even discover such an exploration is in line with—and possibly overlapping—other similar "paranormal" investigations into both modern and ancient "religious," "spiritual" and otherwise "occult," "alien" or "UFO" sightings and encounters.

"Verminology" material suggests a literal and biological interpretation of dragons—even if there is some inner spiritual or metaphysical component involved. While, few may take it seriously, one key attribute described in many diverse sources Pamela Blanpied calls "mimicry"—meaning a dragon's ability to "mime" or camouflage with its physical appearance, literally meshing with or blending into the land's natural terrain. Similarly in the D&D dynamic, an ancient dragon may ascend as a "Guardian" at the end of its lifespan, leaving a physical body that absorbs into and becomes a part of a specific area of land—often a geographical type meeting the alignment of the dragon's element: hills, forests, mountains, caves, &tc.—all of which take on an anthropomorphic appearance or carry some aspect of dragon-like appearance in their features afterward. Other semantics are also employed in Verminology, such as "Dragon Rades"—attacks on livestock and agricultural fields— phenomenon that is just as often attributed to aliens and UFOs. It becomes clear that once we know what to look for, there is evidence of the "Dragon Legacy" everywhere around us since the beginning of time!

The ORIGINAL 1996
DRACONOMICON
OF MERLYN STONE

*This is a transcript of the original
Draconomicon: Sanguis Draconis Report
developed by Joshua Free in 1995
and released in 1996 underground,
writing as Merlyn Stone, and
preserved here for posterity.*

DRACONOMICON: OVERVIEW
—ORIGINAL 1996 REPORT—

Our familiar word *"Dragon"* is derived from the Greek word *"drakon,"* which is mirrored in the Latin *"draconis"* and the Celtic *"draig"* &tc. In the motion picture *"Dragonheart,"* the main character is named *"Draco"*—after a constellation of stars that at one time dominated the northern sky, now replaced by the Great Bear.

In the Babylonian "Epic of Creation"—more recently discussed extensively in the Mardukite Core or "Necronomicon" Cycle by Joshua Free--we are informed about the most ancient dragon, first appearing as TIAMAT. Then, after much quarreling "in the family," MARDUK—thought to be TIAMAT's son—killed her. MARDUK then reigned as supreme ruler of the Universe, using half of her body to form the earth and the other half for the sky. These beliefs coincide with most dragon traditions, particularly the concept of equating the earth planet with the "body" of a primordial dragon.

Throughout classical Greek accounts, we are given stories of seven-headed dragons called "Hydras" and entire dragon-like races of Ladons, Typhons and the notorious Titans. Elsewhere in Europe we find the name "Titania" given to a "Faerie Queen of Elves" (alongside a consort named "Oberon"). The demonization of the sacred image of the Dragon coincided with the rise of orthodox Christianity—particularly as represented in their own sainted personas, like St. George and St. Michael, that became iconic heavenly ordained "dragonslayers."

BUT... WHAT IS THE DRAGON, REALLY ???

This is a difficult subject for some people since there appears to be no living examples of the classical dragon existing in society today. There is, however, a very real draconic energy present on this planet, it just does not always manifest in the manner that we might assume a dragon to be. In fact, the ancient Druids viewed the entire natural system of the earth as "the dragon" and the magnetic lines that run across the surface are even denoted as "dragon lines."

It would also appear the case that significantly higher forms or concentrations of draconic energy are present at specific locales, particularly places like Stonehenge, places where the naturally occurring energies were actually recognized and then harnessed by constructing specific monuments designed to literally divert, tap and/or redirect these currents of energy. Naturally such concepts continue to baffle traditional historians and academic archaeologists as to the "why."

One classical depiction that emerged during my research—on a canvas painting of all places, actually—displays a group of white-robed Druids at Stonehenge worshiping a giant dragon. And, perhaps here, we begin to see a misconception emerge concerning what many interpret as deification and "primitive worship" of these beings and images. This is actually something too often misinterpreted concerning pre-Christian and even Gnostic ideals presented to the mainstream.

It is thought that the consciousness of fire or "fire drakes" were actually summoned (or conjured) for "fire festivals" occurring during the precession of the "wheel of the year"— observed as the "pagan" calendar of seasons. These "drakes" were believed to possess an individual consciousness manifestation because of the wizard or mystic summoning them forth. Some believe that the dragon is always present and manifests in reality because it shares the same energy pool as the planet. Others believe that the dragon is merely a symbol or representation of the universe, its understanding via magic and the power accessible from using this knowledge.

THE "BODY OF THE DRAGON"...

Each magician, priestess or Dragonmaster should maintain a personal "Book of Pheryllt" or "Book of Shadows" (or some similar blank-book of individual design). This is a valuable resource for both designing your personal dragon rites and documenting the resulting experiences. Traditionally, people think of "Book of Pheryllt" or "Book of Shadows" like a underwear or other very personal item that is kept out of sight and safe from unauthorized usage.

The energy, power and presence of the Dragon makes itself known to the Dragonmaster in a number of different ways and this force may not always lend itself to the appearance of a blatantly physical manifestation.

One of the key ingredients for ritual, ceremonial or other practical work with the dragon current is a resinous incense known popularly as "dragon's blood." The numbers 0, 1, 2, 3 and 4 all seem to have significance in the glyphs, signs and rites related to the dragon.

Furthermore, beyond acquisition and use of dragon's blood for rituals and meditations, modern revival Dragonmastery requires the design and creation of a "Draconian Altar"; becoming fluent in ways of the Dragon; befriending the dragon (and the earth); caring for the dragon (and earth) and finally defending the dragon (and earth) as its Guardian.

THE "DRACONIAN ALTAR" ...

The "Draconian Altar" is a sacred altar or table containing the important symbols and icons of the dragon and/or personal power symbols of your own choosing. It can even be chiseled onto a any shaped wooden board—preferably triangular or square—and then supported by large stones or tree stumps. Making a "board" versus a "table" allows for portability if working remotely outdoors where the dragon may be reached.

If your sacred dragon space or "nemeton" is regularly indoors (in your home)—due to the requirement of living in an urban city—you can easily arrange all these things as mentioned to suit your needs and practice there too. It is of utmost importance that time is taken to reach the dragon in the natural state (Green World of Nature) to achieve the desired results. There is really no right or wrong way (so long as it is successful) in going about this so long as the necessary elements of the dragon are met. The following is an example I saw being used in a dense forest. The practitioners personal altar board had the following symbols etched onto it: Sword of Truth, Oak Leaf, Pentagram, Dragon's Eye, Stars (multi-pointed), Crescent Moon, Oak Tree, Sun, Mars glyphs and Aries signs.

THE "WAYS OF THE DRAGON" ...

Principle philosophies of the Dragonmaster—or "Ways of the Dragon"—coincide with what are usually referred to as the "Welsh Triads" such as:—

3 Spiritual Instructors of Mankind:
Mastery of Self
Mastery of the World
Mastery of the Unknown

3 Things Making Rebirth Necessary:
Failure to obtain Wisdom
Failure to attain Independence
Clinging to the Lower Self

3 Things Always Requiring Control:
The Hand
The Tongue
Desire

3 Signs of Cruelty:
To Needlessly frighten an Animal

To Needlessly tear at Plants & Trees
To Needlessly ask Favors

3 Signs of Compassion:

Understanding a Child's Need
Not Disturbing a Sleeping Animal
Lending Aid to Strangers

3 Things Never to be Revealed:

The Disgrace of a Friend
Injurious Truths
The Secrets of the Priesthood

3 Things Found Everywhere:

God
Truth
The Circle of Knowledge

3 Things Never to be Understood:

The Plane of the Existence of God
The Love of God
The Duration of Eternity

3 Like Characteristics of God & Dragon:

Complete Life
Complete Knowledge
Complete Power

3 Laws of Mastery:

To Know
To Dare
To Be Silence

TO "KNOW, DARE & KEEP SILENT" ...

If each of these facets (listed in the title) can be followed, then
supreme wisdom and fluency in relevant mystical arts can fol-

118

low. Quite simply this includes knowing or learning the ways of the "Druid," daring to use these ways and finally the silence (secrecy) concerning their use. Surely if you went to someone on the street and said: "Hey, I'm going to go summon a dragon tonight!"—they would probably either think you were crazy or harass you as a "devil-worshiper"...or *both!* And naturally, if you are following this tradition in self-honesty, you are not.

TO KNOW—If you are reading this book right now, then you are acquiring the "know." The "knowledge" itself is the first part of its own triad, "3 Keys of Mastery," which should govern true pursuits by the Dragonmaster:—

True Knowledge
True Strength
True Wisdom

Knowledge and strength are really the only factors in an individual that are often "judged," "gauged" or "measured" when compared to age, to other people, &tc. Knowledge is simply taught and gained as time goes on—though its pool can be tainted by false knowledge and false beliefs used to interpret knowledge and experience. Personal strength—physical, emotional, psychological—in a sense, also grows with time, though it follows its own cycles of peaks and valleys, all of which may be affected by mundane and worldly matters.

True wisdom can never be truly taught or "relayed" to another—it can be introduced or even suggested via some related pathway, but anyone who can guarantee to bring you or grow "wisdom" in you verbatim is boasting, deluded or dishonest. They may not even know it—for they have failed to understand that they remain within the limitations of their own physical existence and cannot truly "share" the experience with another who will undoubtedly interpret the same stimulus in a different way. This is really basic psychology and it is inescapable. Even assuming a genuine gnosis or experience by an individual, the communication relay of the same without discernment does not guarantee the message is understood.

TO DARE—Naturally when people think of the word "dare" they think in terms of: "I *dare* you to do something..." Well, in this case, that's not what it means. It involves only one person —*you!* This path cannot be forced; not even by you. If it is meant for you, then it will come naturally. So if it isn't working for you—or registering naturally for you—then one of three things is happening. Eliminating all of these as potential barriers virtually guarantees success...

a) you aren't meant to be follow the "druid" or "mystic" in this lifetime;

b) you aren't ready to follow your destined path at this juncture of your lifetime;

c) you are still skeptical and don't actually believe in your own abilities to direct personal willpower via the unlimited Self.

The last part—which is self-defeat via self-doubt—is the most common reason why novices in the "magickal arts" today find little success with their work. And a skeptic set out to prove that his own powers do not work will undoubtedly prove this to themselves. Seeing is not believing. I know it sounds cliché and ridiculous in this pop-culture self-help puffball world, but believing and knowing is seeing. That's the way our brain actually works. For example, a "druid" will come into contact with, tap and channel what they *recognize* and what would otherwise be unseen and unobservable elemental currents of cosmic energy that are alive and abundant on the planet.

TO REMAIN SILENT—You have so far learned that no matter how much knowledge you attain, it means little if it is not being used. Well, some of this knowledge and wisdom (or your belief in such and self-reliance and self-honesty) can be "taken" from you as well. For example, when you talk to skeptical people about being, for example, a "pagan Druid," they might either belittle your magickal talents or socially "excommunicate" you. Some people will retaliate with mystical (or psionic) abilities thinking negative currents of energy and directing them in anger, using in appropriate imagery, or malicious intentions such as wishing harm—all of which are not conducive to positive energy flow and our Ascension path.

Visualization and mystical abilities (more appropriately "wizardry" and "sorcery" of the physical plane) can be used in self-defense or in "magical warfare," but it really should be a last resort. The best way to avoid the situations in the first place is simply to "remain silent." This is why your work, your personal "Book of Pheryllt" or "Book of Shadows" and all ritual implements are meant to be "secret" and hidden and not left out to be subject to the "reality engineering" of another. I realize, of course, that some pagans, mystics and Druids are younger, minors even, and live with their parents or are subject to some other method of controlled environmentalism. This is not typically a problem if your parents are "pagans" or like-minded to you, but a significant amount of teenaged practitioners do not actually have such for parents.

In this case, it is their right, of course, as your wards and guardians to be in a position of direct control. Particularly of your environment. It can be very frustrating for a parent that is not educated in semantics and history and true lore to find our that their child is getting involved with "witchcraft." Even if this is not literally the case—for example, with "Druidism" or some other mystic school with bright aspects—it is often too difficult to make these distinctions clear to uninitiated. One finds that it is simply better to "not talk about it." I would recommend, however, that one actually allow their parents to read these works in self-honesty so that they might understand that in this form it is not so much about giving over the control of your life or "soul" to some foreign entity, but on the contrary is about taking back the ability to function and think self-honestly in a world of depersonalization and misinformation.

Another point: it is a good idea not to pretend to be an expert in these matters precariously. This is a tendency that follows the excitement of getting involved in secret and esoteric factions of reality. I would also add that such can get you into trouble, not having the right research in front of you or the worlds chosen, especially when going up against "authority figures" in defense of these inner traditions.

THE DRAGON & THE "NEW WORLD ORDER" ...

It is surprisingly not hard for many mystics, wizards, druids, druidesses, priestesses and magicians to operate in the modern world. The networking capabilities available now are nothing like they were when the New Age Movement began to "move." However, even among "free people" it would appear that there is much separation based on the cultural and traditional alignment one has based on supposed "systems." For example, an estimated mere 20% of neopagans might consider themselves "druids."

People seldom like to think about the "New World Order" and other seemingly "apocalyptic" subjects that frequently plague the modern world being what it is and times being what they are (as experienced on this plane of those programmed to experience it—for as we know all time and space is oneness).

I remember being asked once when I thought the world was going to end and I answered with, "Isn't the world always ending, with the known world giving way to a new one rising each moment?" They didn't go for it and I tried to explain that I don't necessarily even think the "world" as in "material existence" is in immediate danger of ceasing to exist and being sucked into nothingness (though possible)—but that doesn't mean that the systems that we have come to know as "our world" could not be ended and those who are already being drawn to these more rural and naturalistic functions may be called into service.

Though there are many stumbling points toward the unification of the metaphysical enigma and contemporary science, the Law of Conservation—made famous by equations of Einstein—show evidence towards the idea that creation never simply "dies" out. It changes forms, surely, and can transmute into something uninhabitable for existing conditions, but it is not "gone." Although the concept of man's apelike evolution as given in the history books is completely bogus when compared to more recent evidence and ancient tablets concerning the ANUNNAKI (and similar beings) but the idea of "continuing evolution" is what causes things to change and "evolve" over "time"—and this is how we are programmed to judge "time" for we know that "change" constitutes "duration" and the REAL is not changing, but static and constant oneness.

What can we say for certain concerning the durations and evolutions of a continuing planet...?

The conditions are changing for the worse and since the world sits upon the Earth, the condition of the Earth follows. It is a sad thought to be sure, but it is dishonest to say anything other than the blatant truth—knowable to anyone who cares to take a moment to look around. Given the rise of computer automation, the internet and elemental and climatic instability, it would seem to be just a matter of "time" before...

BUT...

What if the the true "Guardians of the Earth" culled by Nature, who remained secret all this while allowing the program to run itself out were to rise again?

What if the Druids were to return as the proper "Guardians" to protect the Earth against man?

What if the loss of this spiritual sovereignty of the land is a direct cause of things being as they are?

What if ...?

THE TRUTH AGAINST THE WORLD

THE PERSONAL QUEST FOR TRUTH

Truth is the essence of life. Truth is the unseen power that governs all things. Truth is the key to unlocking the secrets of the universe. But in the material realm, truth becomes subjective in experience as no two people appear to share the same 'truth'. It is through the understanding of our 'personal truth' that we might better understand the nature of ourselves and why we think, feel and act the way we do.

It is written that if you try to understand the universe, you will discover nothing at all, but seek to understand the self and there alone lies the Great Key to the mysteries of all creation.

KNOW THYSELF

The wise instruct us many times to: know thyself—and those two simple words have meaning of utmost importance here. What he meant was that by understanding human nature, all else that could be desired to know, would fall into place.

What many Druids today do not grasp is that before one seeks to know about trees, rocks, animals and other worlds, that they should first come to know themselves. Humans are like a collage of what could be labeled mind, body and spirit, which are simultaneously connected and separate.

SCIENCE vs. SPIRIT

Contemporary systems of science do not really understand the multifaceted aspects of humans because science is only programmed with the ability to establish physical and mundane basis for phenomenon and existence.

For science, man is only a brain; the mind is essentially nonexistent.

The brain is programmed to be a construct limited to the physical reality of existence. The mind, on the contrary, is not a physical form and is full of unlimited potentiality. It is only through Truth that we are able to unlock the unlimited power of the mind. Because of conditioning, the thirst for the quest for the Truth, and the ability to perceive it clearly, can be lost with age.

INEFFABLE TRUTH

I point out here semantic differences between "Truth" and "truth." There are "truths" all around us—but they are composed by man, built upon the language structure and definitions entangled together to provide arbitrary meanings.

In youth, a child has yet to be conformed to this semantic level of 'truth' and it is at this point that they might be unconditionally brought to recognize reality self-honestly for the remainder of their life.

PERFECT BALANCE

The path to the Truth is not necessarily one that is focused on 'perfect balance' of forces in the material world—in fact, on a physical level this idea of perfect balance can never be attained.

A Druidical doctrine exists that explains that the human spirit needs a 'constructive imbalance' to grow, whereas true 'balance' is actually 'static' and promotes stagnation of energy.

When the time comes for you to be 'perfectly balanced' you will not be able, or have need to, exist in the physical world, which is everything but static and unchanging. All manifestation is in some state of 'imperfection' on a 'spiritual' "level"—being fragmented from the ALL into a condensed material existence.

SEMANTIC ISSUES ON THE QUEST

One step often missed on the quest for truth is that one is

even forced to analyze what "Truth" means. How can you know you have found the Truth if you don't know what it is? Likewise, how can you quest for something you don't know? We must determine what is true and how we can know it to be true.

Can we turn to a man-made "artificial" knowledge to distinguish the truth? No, because it is the man-made truths that limit us in our programming and place barriers on what we are capable of understanding socially.

SEEK AND YE SHALL FIND

Many believe knowledge can only be gained through direct physical and personal experiences—but we also find that this is not the case.

It is said that Truth can be found in the unity of 'experiencing, studying and knowing' all things, but the Truth may not be found in any one of those three things.

Truth may be gained or at least brought closer to your reach through what Socrates called "Right Action" and philosophers and mystics often refer to as the "Right Way." This is living in accordance with the natural forces of the universe and by one's true and self-honest intuition.

> "Men have always gone to their graves preaching their own truths; yet the sun still rises."

We must understand that "beliefs" will come and go, religions will open and shut, civilizations will rise and fall but the ineffable Truth of All Thing will remain unchanged.

SOCIAL PROGRAMMING

Holding on to tightly to man-made truths will cancel out what is real because this type of artificial truth programming seeks immediate dominance, but will fade, leaving its believer in "darkness" trying to grasp on whatever will hold them. Another man-made truth program will be there to replace the first and so on.

RITUALISM

Many interpret the search for truth, or this type of philosophy or Druidry as a magic – and in many ways it is , but 'practical magic' and ritualism is merely an 'outward' expression of the 'inner' search for "Truth," or at least they should be. So, in order to gain a 'peaceful' environment we must radiate peace from within—*like attracts like.*

THE TRI-FORCE

The methodology of questing for Truth as a 'tri-force' is existent in doctrinal lore of the Ancient Druidic Council—which sought all Truth in Knowledge as comprised of three aspects:

Strength, Wisdom and Compassion.

To attempt to reach the Truth while on the physical plane is to stand on a ladder delicately balanced and composed of many far-reaching aspects. Skip one step, and you fall backwards.

Misinterpret your foundation, and your ladder will not balance. Seek the false truths, and your ladder will be left leaning against the sky with nothing of substance to hold it upright.

...and when the student is ready,
the teacher shall appear.

DRACONOMICON
APPENDICES

ThE PRIMEVAL DRAGON* —APPENDIX A—

The first creature spawned from out of the abyss—the *Cosmic Dragon*—to whom the Sumerians would give no less a title than: "Mother of All Creation." In Hebrew, the word is *"tehom,"* meaning "the deep" or "primordial sea," by which this force receives recognition in the Semitic Genesis. In an infinite universe not yet manifest, the "primeval dragon"—TIAMAT —is the "first cause" made by the Absolute, the first fragmentation from wholeness and oneness into existence—the "Law of ALL" put in motion.

In most ancient mythology, the *primeval dragon* is personified as the "Mother of All Creation." This force, identifiably female, is credited with creation of the other "gods," including all corporeal spirits visible on earth in ancient times as the *"Anunnaki."* This belief found its way into modern "New Age" theories explaining physical aspects of the gods as "reptilian" in nature, descended from a *"Great Cosmic Dragon."* By definition, all existences fall under this *"Cosmic Law"*—all existences are extensions of the same *"Universal Agent."*

The essence of wholeness (or duality in wholeness) is represented in the Mesopotamian pantheon as "divine unions" or couples. Both the male and female aspects are seen as reflections of as one—though like the physical sexes manifest of man, they are divided for our interpretation as being "god" and "goddess." Depending on which tablet sources are used,

---

* Excerpted from *Mardukite Liber-50*, appearing in *"The Sumerian Legacy: A Guide to Esoteric Archaeology"* and the anthology *"Gates of the Necronomicon: The Secret Anunnaki Tradition of Babylon"* edited by Joshua Free.

the deeds and attributes of one are often placed on the other, demonstrating that the full qualities are complete only when paired. For this reason, early scholars examining the Creation tablets mistook ABZU (the Abyss) as the literal "consort" of TIAMAT. But after his "death," in the Babylonian account, her husband-partner is listed as KINGU.

Let us be clear, however, that more than ABZU, KINGU or any other primordial name listed on pre-Anunnaki lists of "ruler-ship" in heaven, it is the *primeval dragon*—called "TIAMAT"—that is attributed all active ability of creation in the Universe. As the primal force or "prime mover" of a physical existence that came out of the Abyss, our first "deity" (if we are to call it such) is not only a dragon, but female, and her consort is given the more passive role for the act of creation.

Under the epitaphs *"Nammu," "Mammu," "Mummu," "Mammi"* or *"Mami"* (of which was later assimilated into the Babylonian goddess ARURU, among others), TIAMAT is the "Creator Goddess" and "Mother of All Mortal Life," offering up her blood (or "sand from her beaches") to be mixed with the "Breath of ENLIL" and "Waters of ENKI" for the creation of human life on earth. The "name" of MUMMU is actually evoked in Babylonian magic—the *"Book of Fifty Names of Marduk"*—derived from the seventh tablet of the *Enuma Eliš*. The thirty-fourth name listed is "MUMMU," who is sometimes TIAMAT, but is more appropriately interpreted as her "vizier" or "chief-minister"—the "active messenger principle." From the "Mardukite" perspective, all aspects of the Fifty Names are attributed to the power of MARDUK in *Babylon*—

> "...the power given to Marduk to fashion the universe from the flesh of TIAMAT offers wisdom concerning the condition of life before the creation, and the nature of the structures of the Four Pillars whereupon the Heavens rest."

This active principle—MUMMU—is described both as the "Creator of the Universe" and also the "Guardian to the Gate to the Outside," but is not originally a "power" of MARDUK, by Sumerian standards. Based on what we know concerning Babylonian adaptations of earlier Sumerian literature, the "Fifty Names" adopted by Marduk in their tradition were really names of the fifty preexisting "*Anunnaki gods,*" some of which are actually mentioned in the *Enuma Eliš*, playing active roles during the infamous "war in heaven." It is equally possible, on a cosmological level, that these names reflect some fifty "primary elements" composing the cosmos at its material inception. The Babylonian "*Epic*" describes the turbulent formation of earth and humans from "star-stuff" using symbolism of a violent battle between MARDUK and TIAMAT. Michanowsky queries in "*Once and Future Star*"—

"The great riddle is why the primordial sea, which according to Sumerian belief, brought forth the world around us without conflict or confrontation, had suddenly been recast [in Chaldeo-Babylonian literature] in the image of a vicious demon mother who had to be denounced as a menace to law and order and then cruelly destroyed."

With the rise of later generations of gods, a theme of unseating or dethroning the positions of the original and most ancient pantheon took hold. This dualistic viewpoint is most obvious in Babylon, including later Assyrian offshoots.

We see the first militant acknowledgment of a generational gap between "younger" and "elder" pantheons in the "*Enuma Eliš*," where "elders" are either demonized as "evil," removed from the system entirely, or given only passing mention. Compared to earlier Sumerian beliefs, this dualism would seem artificial, created for the sole purpose of elevating the position of the younger pantheon, observed in Babylon, as the supreme forces in the local universe and thereby usurping their ancestors. What could not be done physically was accomplished in a manner that ruling classes have used since the dawn of history and writing systems: the very alteration of said *history*.

Lore of this rebellion is found in post-Sumerian religious and mystical doctrines that identify with a "good versus evil" motif. We see it in the foundations of nearly all later traditions. From Babylon it spread east to Persia and west to Egypt, where its oldest forms are drawn as antagonistic moral dogmas held by Chaldeo-Babylonians, Egyptians and Zoroastrians. The Semitic traditions also inherited this "dualism," as reflected today in contemporary forms of Islam, Judaism and Christianity—all of which are strongly rooted in opposition and polar worldviews. This is found nowhere in ancient Sumer and seems to attach itself later on to the *Primeval Dragon* icon. It is, perhaps, only loosely based on the "Destruction of KUR," understood by modern Sumeriologists only in relation to other known pantheons, as Kramer does—

> "...the monstrous creature which at least in a certain sense corresponds to the Babylonian goddess Tiamat, the Hebrew Leviathan and perhaps the Greek Typhon."

In the more widely known version of the Mesopotamian "Epic of Creation" [translated fully in *"Necronomicon: The Anunnaki Bible"*] we are given an amazing account of how the patron of Babylon—MARDUK—fights and destroys an "evil dragon," TIAMAT. We are spared no gruesome details of the bloody massacre awaiting her, finalized by an execution-styled beheading. We can see parallels of "god-kings" rivaling Chaos-Dragons in many later mythologies. But, on these ancient cuneiform tablets, this is a dramatic "cosmological" event.

After TIAMAT is slain, half of her ("the head") is used to create the "heavens" ("AN") and the other half ("the body") is used to create the "earth" ("KI")—or, "AN-KI," the manifested universe. Some "astrophysical" interpretations of these tablets inspire belief that the epic describes a "collision theory" for the local solar system, particularly concerning formation of earth and moon.

We must assume that the philosophical minds that so carefully devised the Chaldeo-Babylonian system (which became so important for the Egyptians and other mystical and Semitic cultures) never fathomed that the tablets of their Sumerian ancestors, sometimes predating them by thousands of years, would ever be recovered. It seemed that for a time, evidence for Sumerian civilization did disappear from human consciousness, replaced instead by the Genesis offered by Babylonians and later derived Semitic lore. In fact, they were using the same written writing system, the same pantheon, and many of the same cosmological concepts under varying guises. "Superimposition" at a literary level appeared seamless.

It was not until the late 1800's that "Assyriologists" realized that some of the tablets and artifacts excavated from the Middle East were pre-Semitic—from before the *Akkadians*. It is now clear that "proper" formation and order of the primordial universe was adjusted to meet political and spiritual needs of a tribal people rapidly turned metropolitan, raising the position of their local deity to support a famous and widespread influence of *Babylon*. In this case, the "elder gods" or "ancient ones" are overridden by the "younger gods"—those most most accessible in all global mythologies, usually representing planets of the local solar system in every instance.

Putting the physical cosmology of ABZU and TIAMAT aside—as the *Infinity of Nothing* and the *Prime Cause*—the emphasis of the current discourse is primarily on the pantheistic applications to Sumerian *Anunnaki* lore. It is difficult to determine if this "War in Heaven" among sentient *"gods"* did actually take place or if it was only written about later as propaganda to blot out the significance and contribution of their ancestors. Although not necessarily a moral facet, TIAMAT directly represents the *first existence*—the first separation of wholeness from the All-Source. This, in itself, generates a belief for many, in a "fall from grace" or "removal from the Source"— what is really at the heart of all dualism in global religions.

This is most obvious in Gnostic lore—which views all physical existence as "evil," contrast to purely non-material "Godly" or spiritual existence.

If realizing that we occupy physical bodies in separation, removed from "God" directly, we can understand how the human psyche might demonize the form "first removed" as the cause of our own fragmentation. Our ability in explaining this awareness on various "levels" in no way condones behaviors of the younger generation of gods. But they too, must have experienced the same philosophic and spiritual devastation of this realization—and at an understandably higher degree of comprehension.

Dualistic conflict of "forces" in the universe are a necessary property of its existence in movement, but it is not necessarily subject to the "moral dualism" that humans identify with. Forces are constantly working with and against once another to keep "the organized universe" the way it is—and continually moving to the way it will be. Without this, there is only the static and "Infinite Nothing" existence of the original state of ALL, which we cannot even inhabit and still be separated as a being of Self. Thus, the real "division" is essentially what is visible and what is not visible (from a "human" perspective)— for the infinitude we inhabit contains everything and nothing can not exist. In Sumerian mythology, this is observed in the union or bond of "heaven-earth" (AN-KI) as a singular aspect; as a dual aspect, the seen and unseen aspects of reality; and as a zero aspect, still encompassed in and of the abyssal nothingness. Sumerians depicted this abstract form as a "mountain," the physical "bond" between "heaven" and "earth." Ziggurats were built as a reflection of the same.

Not only does the word KUR mean "mountain," but it appears in the only significant "dragon-slaying" example from pre-Mardukite Sumerian literature. This time, however, KUR is not a cthonic abyssal water-based dragon, but is instead deep in the earth, in the mountain—or in a very literal sense, the mountain (earth) itself. There are three available Sumerian versions of this tablet cycle, each successively more recent in its origination, as the characters change. Kramer conveniently paraphrases the three versions—

> "The first involves the water-god Enki, whose closest parallel among the Greeks is Poseidon. The hero of the second is Ninurta, the prototype for the Babylon god Marduk when playing the role of 'hero of the gods' in the Babylonian Epic of Creation. In the third, Inanna, counterpart of the Semitic Ishtar, plays the leading role. In all three versions, however, the monster being destroyed is termed KUR."

KUR is an obscure enigma for the prehistoric Sumerian pantheistic worldview, which is otherwise orderly and peaceful. Only later with increased human population did disharmony arise, wrought by new traditions of "evil sorcerers" commanding chaotic "demons" of plague and pestilence. But these expressions are merely accelerated entropy in motion—the opposite of growth and nurture. They do not seem to correlate with a dualistic nature of "good versus evil" applied to our lore of the *archetypal primeval dragon*.

This force only appears chaotic due to its infinite expressions of "change" and "birth"—like the amoral explosive emission of life from seed or egg. Some esoteric texts render TIAMAT as the *"Ancient of Days."* In the Chaldeo-Babylonian kabbalistic system—also called the *Ladder of Lights*—a mystic confronts TIAMAT ladder as the "Dweller on the Threshold" or "Guardian of the Gate to the Outside"—as a representation of the "Fear of the Unknown" that blocks progress. In other interpretations of the magical path, it is KHORONZON, the "Dragon of Chaos" encountered in the dimensional ascent of astral pathwork.

Modern mystical encounters with this energy may prove challenging for some who hold onto the more animated depictions of a primeval "Dragon of Chaos." This current of power is rather subtle (or gentle) like the waves of the sea, but they can just as easily turn turbulent when perturbed, not also unlike the waves of the sea.

Anthropomorphic manifestations and astral encounters with a personification of TIAMAT generally reflect her "reptilian" form as a sleek black dragon—though in some lights this is actually a dark blood red hue. Rarely she may assume a humanoid form, almost resembling Semitic lore of "*Lilith,*" but always female, and usually with black hair. In *Babylon*, The "Tiamat Gate" is essentially the "*Gate to the Outside,*" which is to say in esoteric terms: the "*Gate to the Abyss.*"

MERLYN AND VORTIGERN*
—APPENDIX B—

BOOK VI

XVII.

Vortigern, after consultation with magicians, orders a youth to be brought that never had a father.

At last Vortigern had recourse to magicians for their advice, and commanded them to tell him what course to take in which to solidify his power. They advised him to build a very strong tower for his own safety, since he had lost all his other fortified places. Accordingly, he made a progress about the country, to find out a convenient situation, and came at last to Mount Erir, where he assembled workmen from several countries, and ordered them to build the tower. The builders, therefore, began to lay the foundation; but whatever they did one day the earth swallowed up the next, so as to leave no appearance of their work.

Vortigern being informed of this again consulted with his magicians concerning the cause of it, who told him that he must find out a youth that never had a father, and kill him, and then sprinkle the stones and cement with his blood; for by those means, they said, he would have a firm foundation. Hereupon messengers were dispatched away over all the provinces, to inquire out such a man.

---

* Excerpted from *Mardukite Liber-P3*, appearing in *"Pheryllt III"* and the collected works anthology *"The Book of Pheryllt: A Complete Druid Source Book"* edited by Joshua Free; as adapted from the chronicle by Geoffrey of Monmouth in *"History of the British Kings"* (1138).

In their travels they came to a city, called afterward, Kaer-merdin, where they saw some young men, playing before the gate, and went up to them; but being weary with their journey, they sat down in the ring, to see if they could meet with what they were in quest of.

Towards evening, there happened on a sudden quarrel between two of the young men, whose names were Merlin and Dabutius. In the dispute, Dabutius said to Merlin: "You fool, do you presume to quarrel with me? Is their any equality in our birth? I am descended of royal race, both by my father and mother's side. As for you, nobody knows what you are, for you never had a father." At that word the messengers looked earnestly upon Merlin, and asked the bystanders who he was. They told him, it was not known who was his father; but that his mother was daughter to the king of Dimetia, and that she lived in St. Peter's church among the nuns of that city.

XVIII.
Vortigern inquires of Merlin's mother concerning her conception of him.

Upon this the messengers hastened to the governor of the city, and ordered him, in the king's name, to send Merlin and his mother to the king. As soon as the governor understood the occasion of their message, he readily obeyed the order, and sent them to Vortigern to complete his design. When they were introduced into the king's presence, he received the mother in a very respectful manner, on account of her noble birth; and began to inquire of her by what man she had conceived. "My sovereign lord," said she, "by the life of your soul and mine, I know nobody that begot him of me. Only this I know, that as I was once with my companions in our chambers, there appeared to me a person in the shape of a most beautiful young man, who often embraced me eagerly in his arms, and kissed me; and when he had stayed a little time, he suddenly vanished out of my sight. But many times after this he would talk with me when I sat alone, without making any visible appearance. When he had a long time haunted me in this manner, he at last lay with me several times in the shape of a man, and left me with child. And I do affirm to you, my sovereign lord, that excepting that young man, I know no body that begot him of me."

The king full of admiration at this account, ordered Maugantius to be called, that he might satisfy him as to the possibility of what the woman had related. Maugantius, being introduced, and having the whole matter repeated to him, said to Vortigern: "In the books of our philosophers, and in a great many histories, I have found that several men have had the like original. For, as Apuleius informs us in his book concerning the Demon of Socrates, between the moon and the earth inhabit those spirits, which we will call incubuses. These are of the nature partly of men, and partly of angels, and whenever they please assume human shapes, and lie with women. Perhaps one of them appeared to this woman, and begot that young man of her."

XIX.
Merlin's speech to the king's magicians, and advice about the building of the tower.

Merlin in the meantime was attentive to all that had passed, and approached the king, and said to him, "For what reason am I and my mother introduced into your presence?"—"My magicians," answered Vortigern, "advised me to seek out a man that had no father, with whose blood my building is to be sprinkled, in order to make it stand."

"Order your magicians," said Merlin, "to come before me, and I will convict them of a lie." The king was surprised at his words, and presently ordered the magicians to come, and sit down before Merlin, who spoke to them after this manner: "Because you are ignorant what it is that hinders the foundation of the tower, you have recommended the shedding of my blood for cement to it, as if that would here make it stand.

But tell me now, what is there under the foundation? For something is there that will not suffer it to stand."

The magicians at this began to be afraid, and made him no answer. Then said Merlin, who was also called Ambrose, "I entreat your majesty would command your workmen to dig into the ground, and you will find a pond which causes the foundations to sink." This accordingly was done, and then presently they found a pond deep under ground, which had made it give way.

Merlin after this went again to the magicians, and said, "Tell me ye false sycophants, what is there under the pond." But they were silent. Then said he again to the king, "Command the pond to be drained, and at the bottom you will see two hollow stones, and in them two dragons asleep." The king made no scruple of believing him, since he had found true what he said of the pond, and therefore ordered it to be drained: which done, he found as Merlin had said; and now was possessed with the greatest admiration of him. Nor were the rest that were present less amazed at his wisdom, thinking it to be no less than divine inspiration.

Also available from the **JOSHUA FREE** publishing imprint:

MERLYN'S COMPLETE BOOK OF DRUIDISM
a master course in druidry for modern druids
by Joshua Free
contains the complete texts:
—The Druid's Handbook
—Draconomicon
—The Elvenomicon
(Book of Elven Faerie, Elven-Faerie Grimoire, Elven Forest Grimoire)
—The Pheryllt Researches
—Pantheisticon & more!

DRACONOMICON

SORCERER'S HANDBOOK

MERLYN STONE
JOSHUA FREE

The Druid's Handbook

Joshua Free

VAMPYRE'S HANDBOOK

JOSHUA FREE

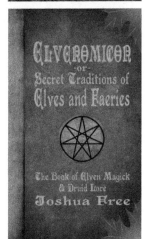

ELVENOMICON
-or-
Secret Traditions of
Elves and Faeries

The Book of Elven Magick
& Druid Lore
Joshua Free

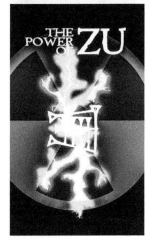

THE POWER OF ZU

SYS𝓘EMOLOGY
The Pathway to Self-Honesty

THE TABLETS OF DESTINY
Using Ancient Wisdom to
Unlock Human Potential
by Joshua Free

CRYSTAL CLEAR
The Self-Actualization Manual
and Guide to Total Awareness
by Joshua Free

- The Core Knowledge of Mardukite Systemology
- Applied Spiritual Tech. of Mardukite Zuism
- Newest Arcane Tablet Interpretations
- Practices of Advanced Spiritual Counseling
- Powerful Spiritual Self-Actualization Tech.
- Self-Processing
- Metahuman Spiritual Evolution for All of Humanity

NABU—JOSHUA FREE ("Merlyn Stone")
Chief Scribe & Librarian of New Babylon
Bard of the Twelfth Chair at New Forest

CPSIA information can be obtained
at www.ICGtesting.com
Printed in the USA
BVHW030937071221
623414BV00001B/117